Character-Building Activities

Teaching Responsibility, Interaction, and Group Dynamics

Judy Demers, MA

D1533916

Human Kinetics

Library of Congress Cataloging-in-Publication Data

Demers, Judy, 1953-
    Character-building activities : teaching responsibility, interaction, and group dynamics / Judy Demers.
        p. cm.
    Includes bibliographical references.
    ISBN-13: 978-0-7360-7206-9 (soft cover : alk. paper)
    ISBN-10: 0-7360-7206-3 (soft cover : alk. paper) 1. Moral education. 2. Activity programs in education. I. Title.
    LC268.D37 2008
    370.11'4--dc22

                                2007048252
ISBN-10: 0-7360-7206-3
ISBN-13: 978-0-7360-7206-9

Copyright © 2008 by Judy Demers

The Web addresses cited in this text were current as of December 15, 2007, unless otherwise noted.

Acquisitions Editor: Scott Wikgren; **Developmental Editor:** Kevin Matz; **Assistant Editor:** Laura Koritz; **Copyeditor:** Lisa Morgan; **Proofreader:** Anne Meyer Byler; **Permission Manager:** Carly Breeding; **Graphic Designer:** Nancy Rasmus; **Graphic Artist:** Tara Welsch; **Cover Designer:** Robert Reuther; **Photographer (cover and interior):** Neil Bernstein; **Visual Production Assistant:** Joyce Brumfield; **Photo Office Assistant:** Jason Allen; **Art Manager:** Kelly Hendren; **Associate Art Manager:** Alan L. Wilborn; **Illustrator:** Argosy; **Printer:** United Graphics

Printed in the United States of America   10 9 8 7 6 5 4 3 2 1

Human Kinetics
Web site: www.HumanKinetics.com

United States: Human Kinetics
P.O. Box 5076
Champaign, IL 61825-5076
800-747-4457
e-mail: humank@hkusa.com

Canada: Human Kinetics
475 Devonshire Road Unit 100
Windsor, ON N8Y 2L5
800-465-7301 (in Canada only)
e-mail: info@hkcanada.com

Europe: Human Kinetics
107 Bradford Road
Stanningley
Leeds LS28 6AT, United Kingdom
+44 (0) 113 255 5665
e-mail: hk@hkeurope.com

Australia: Human Kinetics
57A Price Avenue
Lower Mitcham, South Australia 5062
08 8372 0999
e-mail: info@hkaustralia.com

New Zealand: Human Kinetics
Division of Sports Distributors NZ Ltd.
P.O. Box 300 226 Albany
North Shore City
Auckland
0064 9 448 1207
e-mail: info@humankinetics.co.nz

I dedicate this book to my family for listening to my endless commentary about the progress of the book. Dad, thank you for being my number one fan. You are a true inspiration.

Contents

1 Cooperative Activities   1

2 Developing Self-Esteem 55

3 Reflection Activities 107

Preface

Character-Building Activities: Teaching Responsibility, Interaction, and Group Dynamics was written with the middle school and high school physical educator in mind. However, most of the activities in the book can easily be adapted to younger audiences and used in various curricular areas such as language arts, social studies, and leadership classes. The activities could be an effective resource for anyone responsible for the safety and education of our youth. This may include, but is not limited to, teachers, parents, counselors, and coaches.

The book is divided into three chapters: Cooperative Activities, Developing Self-Esteem, and Reflection Activities. In chapter 1, activities are presented that require individual responsibility and group effort to succeed. While problem solving, participants will learn to be leaders, followers, and compromisers. When young people are given opportunities to look out for others, they can feel a sense of belonging and accomplishment. The first activity in the book, From War to Peace, is a game that shows various stages of growth in society. During the course of the game, participants go from being more aggressive and individualistic to less violent and more cooperative.

In chapter 2, the emphasis is on personal attributes, awareness, and the power of choice. A young person needs to understand that choosing not to react is also a choice. Youth should gain a better sense of who they are and what they value. Once they realize the consequences of particular behaviors, they can work on guided strategies for changing and controlling them when necessary. Participants will be able to examine individual character traits and give personal examples of positive behavior in areas that include honesty, respect, courage, self-control, justice, humility, responsibility, and kindness. It is important for youth to recognize admirable character qualities in themselves, as well as in others.

In chapter 3, young people are given opportunities to communicate their values and strengthen their convictions. The activities in this chapter should stimulate some interesting class (or group) discussions that will reveal what is important in the lives of the young people you work with. It's a great way to celebrate diversity in your classroom or youth group. Allowing young people time to reflect is time well spent. Bringing relevance and validation to the learner is an empowering experience.

Character-Building Activities: Teaching Responsibility, Interaction, and Group Dynamics presents a unique opportunity for youth to learn about themselves through self-discovery. The lessons are relevant to participants; they focus on individual values as well as the contributions that people can make to others. Responsibility for self, social interaction, and group dynamics are interwoven throughout the activities. Self-reflection is an important part of the activities in this book. And sharing and hearing each other's stories can help young people create a healthy community.

Character-Building Activities: Teaching Responsibility, Interaction, and Group Dynamics addresses California State Standard 5 (demonstrate and utilize knowledge of psychological and sociological concepts, principles, and strategies as applied to learning and performance of physical activity).

Acknowledgments

Thank you to all the wonderful people that made this book posible. It was a pleasure to work with such a supportive staff at Human Kinetics. Thank you Scott Wikgren, my Acquisitions Editor, who believed in my work. Thank you Kevin Matz, my Developmental Editor, for all of your tireless work and dedication. You always responded quickly to my many questions.

Thank you to all my students, present and past; you were the motivation for this work. I hope this book will help you realize that you are important and can be instrumental in making this world a better place.

Introduction

Having been a physical education teacher at the elementary and middle school levels for more than 15 years, I have continually been amazed by the diversity of skills and attributes that young people bring with them to class. I am reminded, on a daily basis, that neither motor nor social skills are instinctual; they both have to be learned. As parents and educators, we cannot assume that the necessary skills will develop with maturity.

Those of us who work with young people have the unique opportunity to address and help develop their physical, emotional, and social skills. Neglecting any of these areas can be a compromise to a young person's total health.

At the outset of this school-district-approved professional improvement project, I made a list of positive and negative character traits. I wanted to write a book that would provide various activities for building strong character and social skills. My references come from a variety of sources, which include observations of my own students. Most of the activities in this book are original or are adaptations of existing activities I have seen over the past 20 years.

I learned many things about myself as well as my students while doing my research. I realized that I sometimes make false assumptions about the intentions and behaviors of my students. It cannot be assumed that young people are equipped with proper social skills and strong characters. Children need to be taught these skills and given opportunities to practice them. It's amazing what teachers and youth-group leaders can learn from the young people they work with when they are willing to give of themselves and offer opportunities for participants to share their personal stories. Young people need to feel valued, and they need to know that they can become responsible, contributing members of society.

This book presents activities that provide social-skill development and character-building strategies. Teachers and youth-group leaders, do not assume that children automatically have positive people skills. Knowing the proper ways to interact with others has to be learned. It is not always taught at home and it does require opportunities to practice.

I hope the lessons and activities in this book are an aid to you and the young people with whom you work. I'm sure your investment will pay us all back in positive ways that we can, as yet, only imagine.

We become just by practicing just actions,we become self-controlled by exercising self-control, and we become courageous by performing acts of courage.

—Aristotle

Cooperative
Activities

Being able to communicate effectively and work for a common goal are important social skills necessary for building and maintaining healthy communities. Competition and individual effort are not discouraged in collaborative ventures; a successful team is only as strong as the unity of the individuals on it. Those who work cooperatively learn to value others' worth and to develop compassion and acceptance.

The activities presented in this chapter range from small-group (partners) to large-group (whole-class) format. While problem solving, group members will learn to be leaders, followers, and compromisers. Giving young people opportunities to look out for others can give them a sense of belonging and accomplishment.

From War to Peace

AGES: Kindergarten through adult

EQUIPMENT: Beanbags of various colors (at least four of each color)

PURPOSE: This activity was developed to represent my intentions in writing this book. From War to Peace simulates, in a simplified way, how people in society react to each other with various degrees of tolerance, compassion, and commitment. The activity addresses various stages of behavior ranging from aggression to compassion. The participants experience individual aggression and isolation, group identity and perseverance, and finally tolerance and compassion. As a result of doing this activity, my students have had discussions about healthy and unhealthy environments, fair treatment of the underprivileged, persecution, prejudice, and racism.

PROCEDURE: The goal of the activity is for players to keep moving (stay alive) by having a beanbag stay balanced on their heads or shoulders. There are five stages in this activity. Each stage represents social behavior that ranges from more to less aggressive and from less to more cooperative. A short discussion should occur after each stage. Questions to be asked might include the following:

- What was your strategy during this round?
- What did you notice about other people?
- What comments did you hear?
- How did you feel?
- What might the colors represent in later rounds?
- Does this represent a healthy society?

The leader should time each stage and talk with the group about why some stages lasted longer than others. Ask the participants what each stage might represent in real life.

Stage 1:   Colors mean nothing. Everyone plays as an individual. Everyone tries to flick the beanbag off of someone else, by only touching the beanbag, as they walk within a confined area. If a beanbag falls, the player picks it up and sits down out of bounds. That player did not survive during this round but will play again during the next round.

Stage 2:   Colors again mean nothing. Players are still trying to survive as individuals. This time, while they're walking, they don't flick beanbags off of others: they just see how long they themselves can last. Once a beanbag has fallen, the player picks it up and sits down out of bounds. You may want to set a specified time limit for this round if it lasts longer

than 5 minutes or so. The group leader or teacher might ask questions like the following:

- Did this round last longer than the first?
- Is this an example of a healthy living environment?
- Could a community like this one survive and thrive for a long time? Why or why not?

Stage 3: This time each group is represented by a color. Players try to flick other players' colors off, but not their own team color. Here are questions the leader might ask after this round:

- How did you feel after this round?
- Did you feel more aggressive toward others who weren't in your own group?
- Were you any more energized than in the previous rounds?

(continued)

(continued)

Stage 4: Colors represent the groups again. This time players do not flick others' beanbags off. Instead, the players in each color group try to help their group members survive. If a person's beanbag falls, that person stands next to it with her arm bent and palm up and waits until someone else from the group is able to pick it up and place it in her hand. Once the beanbag is in the player's hand, she can place it back on her shoulder or head and move again. Sometimes the teammate who is helping will lose his beanbag in the process. If no members of a color group are still moving, the group members must pick up their beanbags and sit down out of bounds (as teacher or group leader, you may need to let players know when their entire team is out). Play continues until only one color group is left. Here are some questions you might ask at the end of the activity:

- How did you feel when others ignored you and were not willing to help?
- What did it feel like when you had to walk by others in need?
- What might this scenario look like in real life?

Stage 5: Colors again mean nothing. Everyone is on one team. When anyone has lost his beanbag, he must stop moving and stand up straight with elbow bent and palm up, as in stage 4. Only this time, a player in any color group can rescue any nonmoving player. The object is to keep the whole group moving. Here are questions you might ask this time:

- Does this represent a healthy society?
- Without saying names, what were some of the positive and negative comments you heard?
- Why did some stages last so much longer than others, even with the same number of players?

You can simplify the activity for younger participants by presenting only stages 3 and 5. Discuss friendships, and ask what it means to be a good friend. If you have anyone who is not participating, ask them to be observers. They should pay attention to the noise level, words spoken, and body language during the various stages of this activity.

Life Support

AGES: Grade 4 through adult

EQUIPMENT: 10 balls, 10 poly spots (or dome cones), 20 cones, flags

PURPOSE: In this activity, participants must strategically keep their team-mates moving in order to retrieve all of the balls and place them in their team's circle of cones. To be successful, participants need to work together to keep their team alive. It is important not only to collect the balls but also to rescue teammates who have become prisoners. This allows inactive players to become contributing members who can help strengthen the team.

This is a good cooperative activity. The team that wins is not usually the fastest but is the team that tries to free all of its prisoners, regardless of those prisoners' abilities. It's not uncommon for the fastest runners to become prisoners first; the slower runners and the more passive players often are the ones who keep the game going.

PROCEDURE: A field is divided in half using poly spots or dome cones. There are no sideline or end line boundaries. A circle of cones is set up about 10 feet (3 meters) in diameter and 30 yards (27 meters) from the centerline on each side. At the beginning of the game, each team should place half the balls in their own circle of cones. Before the game starts, each team should meet for a few minutes to discuss their strategy.

Two teams, wearing different-colored flags, each take possession of one half of the field. On each team, two guards are allowed to be no closer than 5 feet (1.5 meters) from the team's circle of cones; all other players need to be at least 15 feet (4.5 meters) from the circle. On the signal to "go" players may run across the centerline into the opponent's territory to retrieve balls and bring them to their own circle. It is advisable to have guards stay near the balls in the circle. A game played without guards protecting the balls usually ends quickly. If a player's flag is pulled while he is carrying a ball, the ball goes back to the circle and the player is a prisoner at the spot where the flag was pulled. Players are allowed to bring back only one ball at a time. Balls that are retrieved from the opponent's territory or confiscated by an opponent must be carried back to the appropriate end line. Players are not allowed to travel into their own circle of cones unless there are no balls for the opponents to pick up. In this case, flags may be pulled, and players become prisoners just outside the cone area.

When teams are on their own sides, their flags can't be pulled. Once a team travels into the opponent's territory, their flags can be pulled, unless they are in their opponent's circle of cones. Once a flag is pulled, a player puts the flag back on and then kneels or sits down and becomes a prisoner at that spot.

(continued)

(continued)

Guards must stay at least 5 feet (1.5 meters) from their prisoners. Players should try not only to steal the balls from their opponents but also to free their team's prisoners. As a teacher or group leader, be sure to emphasize the importance of teammates rescuing their prisoners; this promotes a spirit of cooperation and instills the ideal of sacrificing individual success to that of the team.

To free a prisoner, team members must travel into their opponent's territory and tag the prisoner before their own flags are pulled. (Team members cannot free prisoners while they are carrying a ball.) Freed prisoners must travel back to their own territory, with one hand raised, before continuing to play the game (the raised hand gives them a free walk back to their own side). Once a prisoner has been freed, the rescuer may continue to free others or may try to steal a ball.

Prisoners can be rescued by individuals, as just described, or by a "lifeline." A lifeline is a way for players to save their teammates without becoming prisoners themselves: Players hold hands with others on the same team, forming a chain. One person in the lifeline must have both feet on their team's half of the field, or from within the opponent's circle of cones, but the lifeline can weave across the opponents' territory. No one can pull the flag of a player who is part of a lifeline. All prisoners within reach of the end of the lifeline should

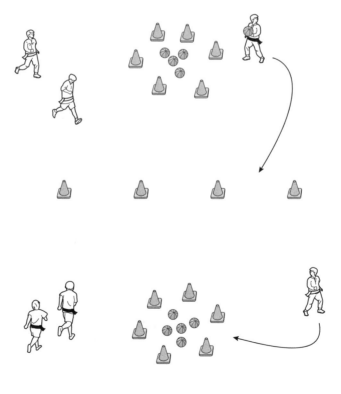

hold hands, if possible, without moving their feet, and should connect with the player in the lifeline who has a free hand. Any prisoner or prisoners saved by a lifeline must stay connected to the lifeline until they are back on their own side of the field; then they may release hands and continue to play.

The ball may be passed laterally or backward to other players whose flags have not been pulled. However, players cannot be facing their own end line and throw the ball backward in their opponent's direction; the ball needs to progress in a forward direction on the field.

The game ends when all of the balls are in one circle or when all the members of one team have become prisoners. If a game ends too soon, by one team bringing all the balls to their end line, you may want to extend it until all players have become prisoners. If players stand too long with a ball in the safety area (within the circle of cones), you may want to incorporate a 15-second time limit rule so progress of the game is not delayed. Once a player has left the safety area with a ball, they cannot bring that ball back to the safety area to avoid being tagged (that is, once players have left the safety area with a ball, they may not bring it back with them to the safety area).

VARIATION: The game can be played indoors, in a gym. Instead of a circle of cones, spread the balls out across the end lines. Make the rule that no one can be saved except by the lifeline. If a lifeline loses its anchor in the opponent's territory, any of the players in the line can be tagged, causing the entire line to become prisoners. Anchors can form from behind the centerline or the end lines. If anchors are formed behind the end line, no one is allowed to hold a ball while freeing prisoners. The lifeline formed behind the end line must weave prisoners back to the end line before disconnecting. Individual players at the end line who don't have a ball can be tagged and made prisoners. Players may strategically use lifelines to protect players running with the ball.

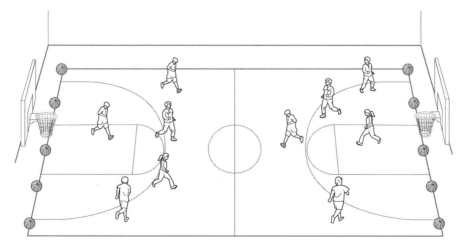

Quick Teach (Peer Teaching Activity)

AGES: Grade 4 through adult

EQUIPMENT: 1 pencil and 1 index card for each pair of participants

PURPOSE: This activity gives participants an opportunity to teach and be taught a simple task, which helps develop their leadership and listening skills and allows them to share a part of themselves with someone else. Learning how to stay focused, isolate important information, and summarize key points are tools for successful learning in all subject areas.

This activity was presented to me at a motivation workshop. I later learned that some large corporations use the activity in their job interview process. Giving interviewees a short time to teach a simple task allows them to demonstrate their leadership and communication skills. For teachers or youth group leaders, it's wonderful to sit back and watch young people come alive with excitement and motivation to learn. I can't think of a better way for people to learn than to be taught by each other. The worst thing I've seen happen when students teach each other is a student teacher becoming frustrated with a fellow student who was off task or confused. However, even that situation might have helped the frustrated student develop compassion.

This is a fun activity to watch. Some of the students in my class who never enthusiastically participated became animated participants. This is a good way for teachers and youth leaders to become aware of participants' interests; in my own experience, I discovered that a shy boy in the back of my class was willing to try break dancing when taught by a fellow student.

PROCEDURE: The young people are grouped in pairs. One person is the "instructor," and the other person is the "student." The instructor is given 3 minutes to teach a simple task to the student. The student should write the numbers 1, 2, 3, 4, and 5 vertically on an index card. As the student is presented with the lesson, she is allowed to write two words next to each of the five numbers. These words should help the student remember the sequence and the details of the activity but should not name the activity. For example, if the student is learning how to throw a Frisbee, one of the numbered items may be "release object," but it cannot be "release Frisbee." Once the instructors have completed the lesson, ask the children who acted as students to demonstrate the activities they learned. When everyone has demonstrated, turn the card over and allow the "students" to become the "teachers."

As a variation on this activity, after each person in all of the pairs has been both an instructor and a student, the activity can progress to include the entire class. The leader should collect the cards from each pair of participants. The leader can choose examples to read out loud to the class. Ask for a volunteer not familiar with the example to act out what they hear. Ask the young people if they can figure out what activity is being taught. If they cannot figure it out, have the original teacher demonstrate the activity.

New Game Development

AGES: Grades 3 through 8

EQUIPMENT: Miscellaneous equipment, depending on student needs

PURPOSE: In this activity, participants have an opportunity to enhance their communication skills and become aware of the special needs of others. Young people become leaders, followers, compromisers, and problem solvers as they work cooperatively to develop a new game or activity.

PROCEDURE: Participants are asked to develop an innovative physical activity that meets the following specifications and includes at least 10 people: There must be at least two kinds of movement in the activity, two or more pieces of equipment must be required, and the activity must accommodate people with special needs. The activity must also have a creative name and theme, and it must incorporate all of the ideas listed in the "appropriate games" category. Appropriate games need to be safe; have simple rules and adequate space; and be fun, challenging, and inclusive for participants of all skill and ability levels.

Before thinking of game ideas, the young people need to be given background information on what makes a good game. They should discuss games or sports they like and tell the class or group why they like them. Comments may include ideas involving action or strategy. Issues regarding diversity and compassion should be discussed. The participants should be given the opportunity to form their own groups; however, no one should be excluded from a group they want to join. I tell my classes that everyone in their group will receive the same grade. Thus, each person in a group needs to be responsible and give his or her best effort to accomplish a collective goal. Although group participation is strongly encouraged, people should be allowed to work as individuals if they are unable to work in a group. Individual effort is discouraged, because the participant will not experience all the skills necessary for cooperative learning such as learning to listen and compromise. If a person working alone decides to join a group instead, this should be allowed. People who decide to work alone must realize that the same amount of work is required from them as from a group.

One person in each group should pick up a stapled packet containing the grading rubric, list of categories ("good game" requirements, equipment available, location, movements, special conditions, and themes), and blank paper on which to design the game and write out the rules.

For the "good game" requirements, ask the participants beforehand to think of a physical activity they like and have them discuss why they like it, as mentioned in the preceding section. If none of the young people mention them, make sure the list includes these characteristics:

- It's safe.
- It has simple rules.
- Adequate space is available for it.
- It's fun.
- It's challenging.
- Participants with various skill levels and abilities can participate.

In the equipment category, all equipment available should be listed. If it's not on the list, it can't be used in game development.

In the location category, make sure all possible areas are listed, such as the volleyball court, the grass field, the tennis court, the gym, and so forth.

The movement section should include a large variety of choices such as run, roll, slide, push, kick, swing, and so on.

Special conditions may include blindness, deafness, or limited or no use of limbs (arms or legs). The special condition needs to be fully incorporated into the game. One group that I worked with decided to develop a game for a special-needs class. On their own, the young people brought in crutches and wheelchairs borrowed from family and friends, and they designed a game for people who couldn't walk or had limited use of their legs. The class loved it and wanted to play it over and over!

Concerning the themes—they should be creative. Some ideas include outer space, under the ocean, and prehistoric times.

Once the game is developed, the child or group teaches it to the rest of the class or the larger group. Part of the group participates while others observe. After 10 to 15 minutes have passed, the teacher or group leader calls the group together to critique the activity. Before the critique begins, the teacher should let everyone know that the only acceptable kind of criticism is constructive criticism. There should be no negative comments made about any person, only suggestions on how they think the activity could be improved. The person acting as the teacher should not take these comments personally. I remember a student, who happened to be my daughter, once very diplomatically telling a game designer that although she liked the game, it might be too physical for some people. The designer immediately took offense and began to yell at my daughter. My daughter responded, "Did you hear me say I liked the game?"

When the activity is completed, the teacher or leader should ask the group what they thought of it. Is there anything you would change? Once the game developers answer the questions, let the participants answer the same questions.

(continued)

(continued)

I've presented this activity to a variety of age groups. I find, in general, that younger children are less inhibited and can more easily come up with creative ideas for games. Once my eighth-grade class realized it was okay to "be a kid again," they had a great time creating and playing their games.

Over the years, I've noticed that many of the games developed are not very creative. During the past year, most of the games I observed involved some form of dodge ball and were aggressive in nature. If you want to see more originality, you might need to make the rule that games should not include dodge ball or have war as the theme.

Another observation I've made is that children who lack good social skills find this activity very difficult. These kids move from group to group trying to find a suitable fit. The problem always has to do with someone else!

After the new-game unit is finished, I ask my students to write in their journals. Students are asked to answer three questions:

- What did you like best about the activity?
- What did you like least about the activity?
- What did you learn about yourself?

Some of the things that students have reported liking include being allowed to form their own groups, creating their own games, and teaching their games to other students. Several students mentioned not liking the fact that groups argued a lot, or that other students didn't listen to the rules when they were being taught. The most common answer to the "What did you learn about yourself?" question was "I didn't know I was so creative."

New Game Development Grading Rubric

Organization (4 pts. possible)

____ Presenters set up their station quickly.

____ Presenters were able to keep the class on task.

____ All presenters were involved in the presentation.

____ Presenters seemed to know what they were doing.

Presentation (4 pts. possible)

____ Presenters spoke clearly, so all could hear.

____ Rules of the game were easy to understand.

____ Presenters checked for understanding (asked if anyone had questions).

____ Presenters showed enthusiasm.

Development (4 pts. possible)

____ The game was safe.

____ The game was fun.

____ The game was challenging.

____ The game had a name.

General Requirements (4 pts. possible)

____ The game involved at least two movements.

____ The game required at least two pieces of equipment.

____ The game included a fantasy or theme.

____ The game accommodated at least one special need.

Participation (4 pts. possible)

____ The class listened to the presentation.

____ The class was eager to try the activity.

____ All the participants were active.

____ The participants were on task.

Summary (4 pts. possible)

____ The presenters were able to describe their outcome (positive and negative).

____ The presenters were willing to listen to others' comments.

____ The presenters were not offended by constructive criticism.

____ The presenters put away all equipment used.

Total points:_____/24 pts. possible

From *Character-Building Activities: Teaching Responsibility, Interaction, and Group Dynamics* by Judy Demers, 2008, Champaign, IL: Human Kinetics.

Ultimate Guard

AGES: Grade 3 through high school

EQUIPMENT: 2 spongy (nerf) balls the size of volleyballs, 4 tall cones, 4 beanbags, 5 poly spots, 12 dome cones

PURPOSE: The purpose of this activity is for team members to protect their castle and royalty and outlive their opponents. The game requires cooperation and compassion for others on the team.

PROCEDURE: Divide the group in half. There should be at least 10 players on each team. A basketball court is the ideal place for this game. To set up the court, divide the area in half using the poly spots. Spread out 6 dome cones at each end line. About 5 feet (1.5 meters) in front of the dome cones, place 2 tall cones approximately 10 feet (3 meters) apart and directly across from each other. Balance a beanbag on top of each cone. These represent the castles.

One team should be on each half of the court. At least one prisoner should represent each team. Anyone not wishing to be an inbound player, where balls may be thrown at them, should be allowed to become a prisoner. Prisoners go behind the opposite end line (behind the opponent's team). Before the game starts, each team should secretly pick two people to be the royalty. The other teammates must try to protect the royalty from getting hit by the ball. Players must also protect their castle from falling (the beanbags from falling from the cones). Ask each team to discuss a strategy before beginning the game.

At the start of the game, the prisoners have the balls (one on each side). Prisoners are not allowed to enter the court or cross the end line or sidelines.

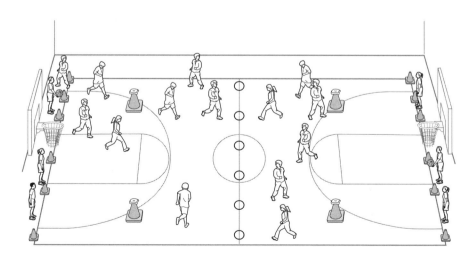

Inbounds players are not allowed to go out of bounds to retrieve balls. The job of the prisoner is to retrieve out-of-bounds balls and throw them to teammates and to catch balls thrown by a teammate over the heads of the opponents.

If the ball is thrown at an opponent and the opponent catches it, the thrower becomes a prisoner (behind the end line of the opponents' field). If the ball hits a player at the waist or below, without bouncing and without being caught, the player who is hit becomes a prisoner behind the opponent's end line. If a player tries unsuccessfully to catch the ball, no matter at what height level, the player hit becomes a prisoner.

When a prisoner catches a ball from an inbounds teammate, all prisoners are free. Each team always needs at least one prisoner to retrieve out-of-bounds balls. The original prisoner may become an inbounds player once another prisoner has arrived. Guards should protect the beanbags and the secret players. If a team's beanbags fall as a result of either an inbounds opponent's throw or accidental bumping by a player, the beanbag is placed under the cone.

The game ends when all players have become prisoners, both beanbags are knocked over, or both royalties have become prisoners. When the game is over, ask players to discuss their strategies. You might ask questions like these:

- Was there a leader, or were there several leaders in the group?
- Did you decide to lead or to follow?
- Was there any disagreement about the original strategy?
- Was your main focus to protect your royalty or yourself?
- Were you more concerned about making the other team your prisoners?
- How did you feel about protecting someone else?
- How did you decide whom to choose for royalty?
- For those of you who were royalty, how did it feel to have someone else watching out for your safety?

Protect the Core (Guard the Center)

AGES: Grades 3 through 8

EQUIPMENT: None

PURPOSE: This cooperative activity requires a group of players to work together to protect a person who is inside a circle they make with their bodies. By moving laterally in unison, group members strive to keep an outside player away from the person in the middle of the circle. If the group doesn't move in the same direction, it will be difficult to protect the inside player. It can be a challenge to move as a group and change directions quickly while watching out for the welfare of someone else.

This is a good drill for basketball; it's a fun way to work on lateral movement, which is often difficult for young people and is widely used in that sport.

PROCEDURE: Participants should get into groups of 5 to 10. One person should be in the middle of a circle of team members who have joined hands, and another person should be on the outside of the circle. The circle is allowed to move laterally, sidestepping left or right in order to keep the tagger (person outside the circle) from reaching the core (tagging the inside person). The circle of players should lean forward slightly and try to keep their backs in front of the tagger.

After the activity is complete, the following questions can be used for discussion:

- Was this activity difficult for you? Why or why not?
- Were you more concerned about your own movement or protecting the person inside the circle?
- How did it feel to be responsible for the inside person?
- If you were the inside person, did you feel you were protected from the outside player?

What Floats Your Boat?

AGES: All ages

EQUIPMENT: One large plastic bowl, straws, tape, Popsicle sticks, marshmallows, paper clips, rubber bands, skewers

PURPOSE: In this activity, participants experience working on a project cooperatively by building the tallest boat possible that will float in a bowl of water.

PROCEDURE: Participants should get into groups of four or five people. No one should be excluded from joining any of the groups. The children in each group should work together to build a boat. All supplies will be placed at a central location. All supplies taken must be used on the boat. Each group is given 15 minutes to complete the

task. The boat is not placed into the bowl of water until the 15-minute time limit is reached. The group that builds the tallest boat that floats for at least 10 seconds wins the game.

The following questions can be used for discussion after the activity:

- What made this activity difficult?
- What made this activity easy?
- Did everyone equally participate? How did you feel if some people didn't help?
- Were you a leader or a follower? Why?
- How was any disagreement resolved?

For older children, you may want to limit the supplies that can be used. For example, you might prohibit the use of tape. You might also have a contest to see who can build the tallest floating boat using the fewest number of supplies.

Bridge the Gap
(Competition Versus Cooperation)

AGES: All ages

EQUIPMENT: 5 carpet squares or poly spots per team

PURPOSE: This activity encourages teamwork. Participants travel across a "raging river" as quickly as possible by walking on carpet squares or poly spots. If team members think as individuals, rather than as a part of a group, the team's progress will be inhibited.

PROCEDURE: Divide the group into four teams. Four teams face inward, two teams across from two teams, with team members lined up one behind the other in a square formation. Opposing teams should stand approximately 20 feet (6 meters) across from each other. The first person in each team should be given 5 carpet squares or poly spots. The object of the activity is for the entire team to travel to the opposite side of the room (the river) by stepping only on the squares or spots. If any member steps off a square or spot, he must return to the starting point. Players are not allowed to throw the poly spots or squares or to scoot with them while walking. No part of the body can touch the floor. If a player does touch the floor, she must start over at the end of the team's start line.

Teams should develop their own strategies as to how they will cross the imaginary river as quickly as they can. The rules are kept to a minimum. Don't tell the group that they can or cannot step on other teams' markers. See if they come to an effective conclusion on their own. In the first round of this activity, the group leader or teacher should time how long it takes the four teams to cross to opposite sides; each team against the other three. Using the same formation during round two, it should be announced that the entire class or group is considered one team. Time how long it takes the entire group

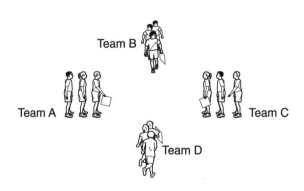

to work together to switch sides, crossing in opposite directions. Allow the group to try this several times. At this point, the teacher or group leader may want to give suggestions.

Once the activity is finished, discuss with the group how they felt about each version of the activity. You might use questions like these:

- Which strategy was most effective for both versions?
- How did the strategy change from one version to the next?
- What version did you prefer? Why?
- Were you a leader or a follower?
- What was the group dynamic?
- Was there more than one leader?
- If disagreements occurred, how were they resolved?
- Did you give any input during the activity?
- Were your suggestions listened to or followed?
- Was everyone of equal importance to the group?
- Without giving names, was anyone ignored or treated poorly? If so, why do you think this occurred? Give a brief summary of what happened.
- Did you stand up for anyone not treated fairly during this activity? If so, how did the person you stood up to react? Were they receptive to what you had to say? What was the reaction of the person you helped? How did you feel about standing up for others?
- Did others in the group ignore poor behavior? If so, why do you think they ignored it?

Ping-Pong Obstacle Course

AGES: All ages

EQUIPMENT: Ping-Pong balls with different numbers on them for each team, 5 cones numbered 1 through 5

PURPOSE: The purpose of this activity is for participants to cooperatively work as a team to move a Ping-Pong ball through an obstacle course.

PROCEDURE: Teams should not consist of more than four members and ten teams. Too much idle time could result in boredom. Too many teams may crowd the field and make it difficult to progress from one cone to another. Team members must take turns and alternately flick, with their index fingers, a Ping-Pong ball to hit consecutively numbered target cones. Example: team 1, player 1 goes; then team 2, player 1 goes; and so forth. Once a player flicks the ball, the next player on the team goes to sit next to the stopped ball and waits her turn. That player must be in a seated position before she can play the ball. If a player hits another player with the ball, the hit team loses a turn. If a player hits another team's ball with his ball, that player receives another turn. Sometimes the strategy may be to purposely hit another player, hit another player's ball, or position the ball so that the seated player blocks the view of the intended target cone. If a team is more than one cone behind all other teams, that team may proceed to the next cone when it is their turn.

VARIATION: Have participants play Ping-Pong crab soccer. Players again are only allowed to flick the ball, but all players must move in crab-walk style. You may decide to let goalies use their whole hands to block goals. Ask the players to come up with creative game ideas using Ping-Pong balls.

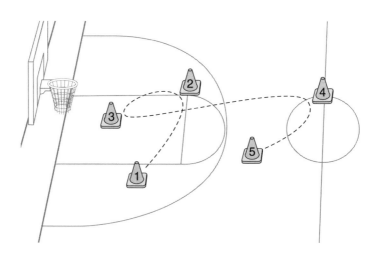

What's the Difference?

AGES: All ages

EQUIPMENT: None

PURPOSE: In this activity, participants learn about the commonalities and differences that exist in the class or group. The activity is a great icebreaker, and it helps participants relate to each other on a more personal level. Having a personal connection with others in the group can help facilitate positive cooperative behavior.

PROCEDURE: Participants should get into groups of five or six people. Groups are given 5 to 10 minutes to discuss things they have in common that are unique; they should try to pick something that they don't think all of the members of another group will also have in common. Have the group members try to find at least three things in common. They might find out that they all have a dog and a cat, or that they all like liver. It's likely that not everyone in another group would be able to say yes to either of those statements. If no other group can unanimously say yes to their statement, that group is given a point. Let each group share one example at a time. When all groups have shared, repeat the procedure for each group's second statement and all further statements.

I'm always amazed at how perceptive students can be about personal appearance and emotions. I've had students realize that everyone in their group was upset with someone, everyone had different-colored eyes, or no one had the same color of socks.

Reverse Polarity

AGES: Grade 4 through adult

EQUIPMENT: 10 poly spots, bases, or carpet squares

PURPOSE: This activity is intended to promote strategic thinking and cooperation. Participants move from positions 1 through 8 to the reverse, positions 8 through 1, without stepping off carpet squares. To accomplish this task, team members need to strategically move and help balance other members in a cooperative manner.

PROCEDURE: Have participants get into teams of eight, and number each team member 1 through 8. Each person should stand on one square or spot. There will be two rows and two blank positions. Team members are not allowed to touch the floor or move the squares or spots. Teammates may help each other with balance. If anyone touches the floor, the team must start over.

To make it more difficult, place students in random order, one at each spot, before starting the activity.

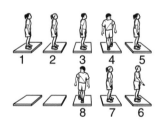

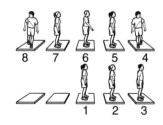

Multiplicity (Tag Game)

AGES: All ages

EQUIPMENT: 2 Nerf balls (or soft throwing objects)

PURPOSE: The object of the game is to work as a group to strategically make everyone a tagger.

PROCEDURE: Two participants with the ball are considered original taggers. The original taggers are permitted to run with the ball and throw it at others who are not taggers. If a tagger hits another player (someone who is not a tagger), at the shoulder level or below, then that player becomes a tagger. Only the original two taggers are allowed to move with the ball. All other taggers may pivot or throw the ball from a stationary position. Taggers should throw the ball either to another tagger who is near a possible target player (nontagger) or directly at a possible target. Taggers who don't have the ball should position themselves next to a potential target player to receive the ball from other taggers. As the game progresses, the original taggers can call for a strategy meeting for all taggers. The game ends when everyone has become a tagger.

This game is difficult for players who think of themselves as individuals first and members of a team second. When the game is over, you may want to discuss teamwork by asking the following questions:

- What does it take to be a good team member?
- Were individuals able to accomplish the task (convert everyone to taggers) without the help of other team members?
- How did the members of the team feel when individuals tried to do it alone?

Five Alive

AGES: All ages

EQUIPMENT: None

PURPOSE: This cooperative activity is an active (running) game where participants need to work together as a class or group to be successful. Open communication and observance of others in the group are important aspects of the game.

PROCEDURE: The group forms a large double circle with at least 5 feet (1.5 meters) between each pair. Five runners are positioned inside the circle. On the signal to go, the teacher or group leader allows 5 minutes for the inside runners to change positions with players in the circle. Runners should count the number of exchanges made during the 5-minute period. Each of the five inside runners should quickly run to and stop behind two players in the double circle. At that time, the inside runner in what is now a group of three should run and stand behind another two players. After 5 minutes is up, ask if anyone didn't get to run at all. Ask how many ran more than 5 or 10 times. Talk about the inequity of playing time.

During a second round, time how long it takes to have each person run at least 5 times. Tell the group that they will have to communicate without talking. The group should try to accomplish the task as quickly as possible. Give the group a second chance to better their record. Try a third round where the participants have to communicate in a different way—they might hold up fingers designating the number of turns they've had, or clap their hands.

After the activity is finished, you might use these questions for discussion:

- How did your strategy change from round 1 to round 2?

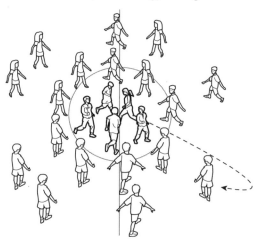

- How motivated were you during each round?
- How did you feel during each round?

It may be a challenge for some young people to communicate nonverbally. You might relate this experience to someone trying to communicate with others in a foreign country and not knowing the language. It can cause anxiety and frustration.

Bystanders Unite (Anti-Bullying Activity)

AGES: All ages

EQUIPMENT: 10 pennies (coins) and vests

PURPOSE: The purpose of this activity is to make young people aware of individual rights and the moral responsibility they have for others who are being bullied.

PROCEDURE: The class or group is divided into vested players and non-vested players. The vest to nonvest ratio should be 1 vested player for every 8 to 10 nonvested players. The object of the game is for vested players to tag nonvested players, forcing them to give up their coins. Nonvested players should work together to avoid giving up their coins. To begin the activity, all vested players should turn their backs to the rest of the group and close their eyes. The teacher or group leader should randomly hand out 1 penny (or some sort of coin) to 10 players without vests. All nonvested players should close one hand, whether or not they have a coin. Once play has started, nonvested players should randomly switch (or pretend to switch) coins from one nonvested player to another. Once a nonvested player is tagged, he must open his hand and show that it's empty or give up the coin if he has one. That player then resumes play with a closed hand. Once a vested player retrieves a coin, she turns it in to the leader. If a coin is dropped, it automatically goes back to the leader to avoid potential injury.

When the activity is over, ask participants the following questions:

- What is a bystander? (Give an example if participants don't know the answer.) What is the responsibility of a bystander?
- Who might the vested players represent? (Explain that these are people who try to take something away from others.)
- What is a bully? Who do bullies target?
- Can bystanders making a stand against bullies make a difference? Give examples.
- How could you stop your friend from bullying others? Give examples.

I once had a conversation with a class before starting this activity on bullies and bystanders. Someone in the class described the bystander as someone who has no power, and the bully as the strong person. I told the class that bystanders should not put themselves in danger but that there are accept-able ways of helping those who are being bullied. I suggested that letting a responsible person know what is happening is a good first step, and I pointed out that bullies prey on those who are weak and that bystanders united can create a strong defense against bullies.

Reach Out

AGES: All ages

EQUIPMENT: 3 hula hoops, 10 beanbags, and 5 poly spots (More equipment may be needed for larger groups or larger playing areas.)

PURPOSE: This game develops participants' awareness of the value of working with others as opposed to trying to accomplish something on their own. The object of the activity is for a group of participants to collect beanbags scattered on a court while standing on a poly spot, in a hoop, or connected to an anchor person in a hula hoop.

PROCEDURE: Use an area about the size of a basketball court. Vary the size depending on the number of people involved. All players, poly spots, and hula hoops must start behind one end line (the start line) and travel to the opposite end line. Beanbags are scattered throughout a designated area. On the signal to go, players must work out a strategy to position the equipment so that all of the beanbags can be collected. The activity is over when all beanbags, equipment, and players cross the end line.

Neither beanbags nor equipment can be thrown. Only one player is allowed on a poly spot at a time. There is no limit on how many people can stand inside the hula hoop. Hula hoops can be used as anchor points. Players inside the hoop can join hands and extend a line outside of the hoop as long as the anchor person remains in the hoop. Hoops and poly spots can be moved as long as everyone remains on a poly spot, in a hoop, or connected to an anchor player in the hoop. If a person steps off the poly spot or out of a

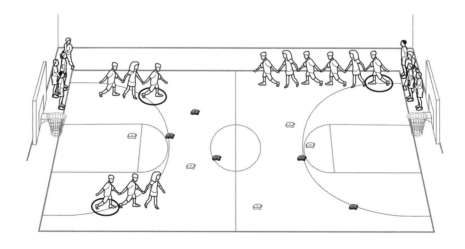

hoop, that person must leave any equipment collected at that spot and return to the beginning to start again. If a chain is disconnected, those disconnected must leave any equipment collected at that spot and return to the beginning to start again.

You can divide a large group into two teams and have each team start at opposite ends of the playing area. (The game is more challenging when opposing teams are crossing paths.) The two teams should have different-colored beanbags that they need to pick up along the way. The team that crosses the end line with all its beanbags and equipment first wins the game.

This game can reveal the various personality traits of your young people. There are those who look out for themselves and those who look out for the group. In one of my classes, I had two students who were very confident in their ability to complete the task. They were going to race ahead of the group and single-handedly collect all of the beanbags. These two students took all of the hoops and left the rest of their group behind. Their strategy didn't work very well; they did collect several of the beanbags, but they stranded themselves in the middle of the playing field. Their teammates had to use the poly spots to rescue them and retrieve the hoops. The students were humbled, and the other team finished way ahead. When the game was over, we had a good discussion about the strength of a team.

Catch Me Being Good

AGES: Grade 3 through high school

EQUIPMENT: Cards or poker chips labeled with positive character traits

PURPOSE: This activity provides an interactive way for young people to identify and share positive character traits.

PROCEDURE: This is a tag game that starts with one person being "It." At the beginning, the person who is It (the tagger) turns his back to the group. The teacher or group leader hands out positive character trait cards (or chips) randomly to several participants. Once the cards are distributed, all players close one hand to make it difficult to see who has the cards. On the signal to go, players scatter in a designated area (a basketball court is a good size). Nontaggers should give cards (or pretend to give cards) to other players. When the tagger touches someone, that person is to open her hand. If she has a card, she gives it to the teacher and becomes an additional tagger. If she doesn't have a card, she closes her hand and continues to play. The round ends when all players have become taggers.

Suggested labels for cards or chips are:

compassionate

trustworthy

friendly

dedicated

disciplined

tolerant

caring

courageous

honest

fair

As a wrap-up to this activity, ask the young people to share their character traits. They should define each trait and give an example. You could extend this activity by asking the players to act out their character traits and having the group guess which traits are being acted out.

When you apply the "catch me being good" philosophy to your everyday teaching and other life situations, the positive experiences that can come out of it might surprise you. Here's an example from my own experience.

My school has implemented a "character trait of the month" activity. Teachers are to look for students (or other teachers) who model a particular positive character trait. At the end of the month, students who have been nominated are called out of their classes. They are honored, and they receive a certificate and a dog tag with the character trait listed on it. Their picture is then displayed in a cabinet near the front office. During the "respect" month, I nominated a boy in my class whom I'll call Tommy. Tommy is autistic; he is easily angered and often isolates himself from the rest of the class. He rarely speaks to anyone.

One day my class was working on volleyball drills, which are similar to a volleyball game but are played on a tennis court. During the drill, one student throws the ball to each of the other students, who stand side by side in a line in front of the student throwing. The idea is for the thrower to toss the ball high enough so members of the team can get under it to make a high set back to the thrower. One girl was having difficulty tossing the ball accurately. Some of her teammates began laughing at her. Tommy immediately came to her defense and said, "Leave her alone; no one is perfect." I was amazed that he not only spoke out but was perceptive enough to be aware of the feelings of others. That's why I nominated Tommy for the "respect" award. A week or two later, Tommy came up to me and said, "You nominated me for an award." He had a trace of a smile on his face. It was the first conversation we'd had in which he wasn't telling me something negative about someone else in the class. Since then we've had several more conversations, and he's shared personal stories about his family life with me.

If you're a teacher or a youth-group leader and you want to see the good side of the parents you interact with, catch their children being good. Correspondence with parents shouldn't be limited to communicating negative news. I'll never forget one of my child's college professors. This teacher found the time to acknowledge my child's effort. He told my husband and me that we had raised an amazing daughter who was responsible and compassionate and that she was a positive asset in his class, contributing to the group on a daily basis. He went on to say he was sure that as she continued to mature, she would make tremendous contributions to the world throughout her lifetime, and that we must be truly proud of her. The professor's praise for my daughter really made my day! His letter also had a strong effect on my daughter, and she will never forget him.

Make It Right

AGES: Grade 3 through high school

EQUIPMENT: Cards or poker chips labeled with positive and negative character traits, and vests for taggers.

PURPOSE: This activity provides a fun, active way to identify positive and negative character traits. In addition, children have the opportunity to describe how a negative trait can be changed to a positive trait.

PROCEDURE: This is a tag game that starts with a ratio of approximately one tagger to every five participants. At the beginning, the taggers turn their backs to the group. The teacher or leader hands out positive and negative character trait cards (or chips) randomly to several players. Once the cards are distributed, all players close one hand to make it difficult to see who has the cards. On the signal to go, all players scatter in a designated area (a basketball court is a good size). Nontaggers should give cards (or pretend to give cards) to other players. When the tagger touches a player, that player is to open his hand. If he has the card, he gives it to the tagger, who takes it to the teacher. If the tagged player doesn't have a card, he closes his hand and continues to play.

A player who has a card with a negative character trait on it must give the teacher a suggestion for how to make it positive before she can continue to tag others. If the player can't give such a suggestion, she can solicit help from any other tagger. The round ends when all trait cards or chips are found. Players with vests (taggers) should give their vests to new players.

The teacher or group leader should time each round to challenge new taggers to beat the time of previous taggers. You might want to place a time limit on each round, perhaps 3 or 4 minutes, so that more people will have a chance to wear the vests. It's a good idea to have a wrap-up discussion about each word. Some questions you might ask include the following:

- What is the meaning of this word?
- What is an example of this word?
- How could a person with this character trait affect the lives of others?

It's important for young people to understand that their actions don't only affect themselves. I once had a discussion with my class about wearing safety equipment. In particular, we were talking about the need to wear helmets while riding bikes or skateboards. One student said, "It's my business if I decide to take a chance; it's my life and my body." I asked him who would pay the hospital bills, which might be more than his parents could afford? Who would take care of him during his long recovery period, if he were lucky enough to recover? What kind of emotional and financial burdens might his decision to not wear a helmet place on his family and friends? Obviously, he hadn't thought of these issues.

Possible character traits for the cards or chips are:

Positive	Negative
compassionate	aggressive
trustworthy	dishonest
friendly	cold
dedicated	bored
disciplined	unruly
tolerant	intolerant
caring	boastful
courageous	cowardly
honest	judgmental
fair	argumentative
complimentary	jealous

Character Search

AGES: Middle school through high school

EQUIPMENT: 1 hula hoop per team, and tennis balls marked with a team number (1 number for each team). Example: numbers 1, 2, 3, 4, 5, 6, 7, 8 to represent 8 teams. Also, 1 tennis ball for the entire group, marked with a circled letter that represents a particular positive character trait. An example would be C on a ball to represent compassion and H on a ball to represent honesty.

PURPOSE: This physical activity promotes eye-hand coordination and lateral movement (beyond the midline of the body). According to Dennison (1994), midline movements help to integrate binocular vision, binaural hearing, and the left and right sides of the brain and body. Cooperation and good sportsmanship are necessary to help this chaotic activity run smoothly.

PROCEDURE: In this activity, participants search for and identify positive character traits. The activity needs to be played on a hard surface that will allow the tennis balls to bounce.

Hula hoops should be evenly spaced on the floor to form a large circle (approximately 30 feet [9 meters] in diameter). The first member of each team stands in his hoop with his back to the circle. The teacher or group leader gives each starting team member a numbered ball (not the team's own number). Before the game starts, the players are told to find their team's ball and then find the group's ball (the one marked with a letter indicating a positive trait). Let the players know what letter they are searching for and the word it represents.

On the signal to go, the players who have the balls lightly toss the balls over their heads into the center of the circle. The leader, at the same time, tosses in the special character-trait ball. After tossing their balls, the starting players will turn around to grab one of the bouncing balls. Only one ball at a time can be picked up. If a player doesn't find her own team ball (example: team 4 must find the ball marked 4 and place it in their hoop), that player will lightly toss the ball into the air and search for another. The object of the game is for the starting player to first find her own ball, then return it to her hoop, and then find the special ball and return it to the group leader before the other teams accomplish the task.

Once that round is over, and before the next player starts in the hoop, the group should discuss the meaning of the word representing the character trait. Perhaps examples could be shared. Here are some questions you might ask participants:

- Are there celebrities or other people you admire who exhibit this quality, or the opposite of this quality?
- How do you feel about these people and their actions?
- Do celebrities have a certain responsibility or obligation to be a particular kind of role model?
- Why is the general public so interested in the lives of the celebrities?

Some examples of character-trait balls are:

I = integrity

H = honesty

C = compassion

E = empathy

Clean Up Your Own Mess

AGES: Grades 3 and up

EQUIPMENT: Various-colored beanbags (5 of each color), and 1 trash can or box

PURPOSE: This activity makes participants aware of the responsibility we all have for keeping our environment clean.

PROCEDURE: A trash can or box is placed in the center of the room. One player on each team is blindfolded. After the players are blindfolded, the instructor or group leader spreads the beanbags randomly throughout the room. On the signal to go, the team members who are not blindfolded tell their blindfolded teammate where to go to pick up their team's beanbags and then how to get them to the trash can (the blindfolded teammate must take the beanbags to the trash can one at a time). The non-blindfolded players must stay at least 10 feet (3 meters) away from their blindfolded teammate.

Each team will want to work out a strategy for effective communication with their blindfolded teammate. It may be difficult for the blindfolded player to understand directions if multiple players are screaming at her at the same time. Each team might choose one player at a time to call out instructions. It also might be of benefit to call out the blind person's name before giving a command. For example, "Sandy, right!" or "Sandy, stop!" For safety, blindfolded players should walk with their elbows bent and hands up in front of them to act as bumpers. When a blindfolded player is instructed to bend down to pick up a bean bag, she should do so by bending her legs and keeping her back straight while lowering herself to the ground. Bending over at the waist could

cause collision with another nearby player (the group leader or teacher can help prevent this by not placing bean bags of various colors too closely together), so be careful! If a player touches another player, that player is penalized and has to stand still for 20 seconds. The first player to pick up all her team's beanbags and put them in the trash wins that round for her team.

As a wrap-up activity, you might have one blindfolded person on each team pick up all colors of beanbags. Then you might discuss with the group whether or not the task was completed more quickly when everyone was on the same team and had a common goal.

An optional part of this activity involves asking groups to come up with nonsense words or sounds to represent English commands. The words should not be in a language that currently exists. Being blindfolded *and* not fully understanding the language makes communication and learning more difficult. This aspect of the activity has the additional benefit of helping participants better understand and have compassion for those who have special needs.

At the end of the activity, you might ask the teams these questions:

- What was your team's strategy?
- Did you try to stop other teams from cleaning up the environment?
- What could that represent in real life?
- How did you feel when someone stopped you from doing your job? What could you do about it?

While supervising in the physical education locker room, I'm constantly picking up clothes, shoes, and jewelry that students have left behind after class, not to mention endless trash. When students come back the next day and can't find their clothes, they tell me they were stolen. Needless to say, in most cases they find the missing items in the lost and found. Many lost items are never claimed because they have been too easily replaced.

I've had students ask me where the trash can is when I've asked them to throw away their garbage, yet they have to practically trip over the trash can to get in and out of the locker room! However, it's not just the young who are blind when it comes to taking responsibility for caring for the environment. Irresponsibility is a learned behavior, and many of us—youth and adults alike—forget to "clean up our own messes."

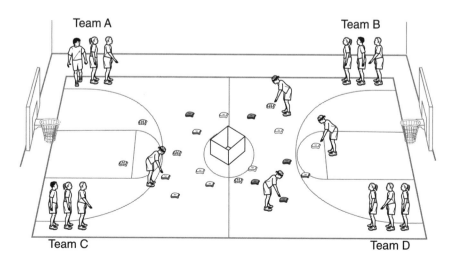

Abolish Aggression

AGES: Grades 3 and up

EQUIPMENT: A clothespin for each child. One side should read "Peace," and the other side should read "Aggression."

PURPOSE: The purpose of this activity is to spread the notion of peace when aggression is a reality. Two groups of players, one labeled Peace and one labeled Aggression, work together to try to convert others in the group to their way of thinking.

PROCEDURE: While the children are seated, the teacher or group leader hands out one clothespin per person. Each child pins the clothespin to a sleeve with the Peace label showing. The leader asks the children to close their eyes. While eyes are closed, the leader taps five children on the shoulder. These children open their eyes and change their clothespins to read Aggression.

Once everyone is ready, all the children open their eyes, stand up, and spread out in a designated area (approximately half of a basketball court for a group of about 30 participants). The leader decides if it is to be a running or a walking game and tells the players to try not to be tagged. On the signal to go, the participants with Aggression on their sleeves should tag those with Peace to make them change to Aggression. The Peace group should tag the participants with Aggression showing and make them change to Peace. The round ends when all players are either Peace or Aggression. If two people tag each other at the same time, neither one should change his clothespin, and both should go on to tag someone else.

When the activity has been completed, you might discuss these questions with your class or group:

- What happened during this activity? Is there anything you would change?
- What was your strategy?
- Why did this outcome occur?
- How did you feel having Peace as your symbol?
- How did you feel having Aggression as your symbol?
- How did you feel if you were converted to Aggression?
- How did you feel if you were converted to Peace?

Then, you might discuss the power of a united front and ask the group questions like this:

- What are examples of historical events or movements that resulted in peace or aggression in society?
- Who were some of the leaders? How did they operate? Why did others follow them?
- What are ways to avoid negative pressure? (You might talk about refusal skills and have the children act out skits to practice saying no effectively.)

Stop the Bully

AGES: Middle school through high school

EQUIPMENT: Blindfolds

PURPOSE: This activity shows participants the power that bystanders working cooperatively can have in stopping the behavior of a bully.

PROCEDURE: At least five objects should be identified and numbered before the start of the game. To begin, two participants are blindfolded. One person is the bully and the other is the victim. The bully and the victim start at opposite sides of the room or designated area. Each person is spun three times before proceeding. The goal for the bully is to touch a designated object in a designated area before the victim or bystanders tag him or her.

One person helps the bully by calling out directions (standing no closer than 10 feet [3 meters] away) indicating how to reach the final destination. The victim (and all future bystanders) has a partner who calls out instructions on how to tag the bully before the bully reaches the destination. No partner should impede the progress of the blindfolded participants. If this should occur, the victory goes to the team whose members didn't impede progress. If the bully reaches the first destination before being tagged, another blindfolded participant enters the game as a bystander. The bystander should start on the opposite side of the room from the bully. The bystander helps the victim tag the bully before the bully reaches the next designated location. The game continues until the bully is tagged by the victim or bystanders or the bully has touched all five objects at various locations.

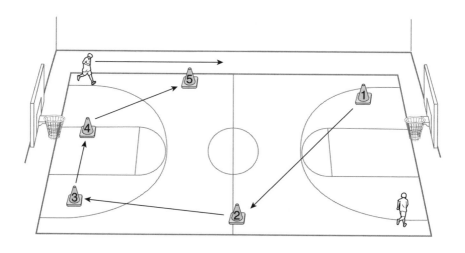

You can use the following questions to guide a discussion with your class or group about the power and the responsibility of bystanders.

- How can bystanders help a victim without putting themselves in harm's way?
- Can a single victim effectively stop a bully?
- What makes it difficult for bystanders to help?
- What gives a bully power?
- Who is the typical bully? How can we change this behavior?

Mixed Bag

AGES: Grade 4 through middle school

EQUIPMENT: 6 hula hoops, a large paper bag, and approximately 30 (8.5-by-11-inch) pieces of paper with a positive or negative character trait written on each. You might ask participants to help contribute a list of traits. Duplications of character traits are permitted. The pieces of paper should be crumpled into tight balls and placed inside the paper bag.

PURPOSE: This cooperative activity helps young people identify positive and negative character qualities in a fun, active way. During this activity, teammates are permitted to give verbal advice to the team member who is participating.

PROCEDURE: Six hoops should form a large circle on the floor, approximately 30 to 40 feet (9 to 12 meters) in diameter. The teacher or group leader scatters the papers loosely in the center of the circle. The first member of each team should stand inside a hula hoop. On the signal to go, the beginning players may take one piece of paper at a time from the center area to their own hoops and may steal one piece of paper at a time from any other team's hoop. No other member of the team can touch the papers or interfere in any way. The only thing that teammates can do, when it's not their turn, is call out directions on where the active player should go. The round ends when one team has five pieces of paper in their hoop. Once the round is over, all

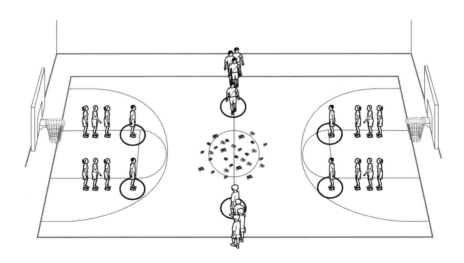

pieces of paper in each team's hoop should be opened. One point is added for each positive trait, and one point is taken away for each negative trait (it's possible for a team to finish first and not win the round). Once the winner is declared, the pieces of paper are crumpled again and are placed back inside the bag to be mixed up and redistributed for the next round.

You can also do this activity as a relay, where one person can take only one piece of paper (either from the center or from another team). Once that person's turn is over, the next person in line takes her turn. Again, the round is over when one team collects five pieces in their own hoop.

When the game is over, you might give one piece of paper to each person. Ask participants who have a negative trait to share it with the group. Ask participants who have a compatible positive trait to share how they might help that person change a negative to a positive.

It's also a great idea to talk to your class or group about the idea that it's possible to win a game but still lose and to lose a game but still be a winner, thereby putting the activity they've just done into a larger context. Point out to the participants how important it is to have the right attitude. Ask them for an example of someone who has won but is not a winner (this might be someone who is not a team player). Then discuss the idea that a person who overcame obstacles or who gave a 100-percent effort might lose a game but still be considered a winner.

Bag It!

AGES: Middle school through high school

EQUIPMENT: 6 hula hoops, a large paper bag, and approximately 30 (8.5-by-11-inch) pieces of paper with a positive or negative character trait written on each. Duplications of character traits are permitted. The pieces of paper should be crumpled into tight balls and placed inside the paper bag.

PURPOSE: This cooperative activity helps players identify positive and negative character qualities in a fun, active way. Teammates work together to place all negative character traits into a bag in the center of the playing area.

PROCEDURE: Six hoops should form a large circle approximately 30 to 40 feet (9 to 12 meters) in diameter (see the Mixed Bag diagram on page 40). The teacher or group leader scatters the pieces of paper loosely in the center of the circle. The bag remains in the center of the circle. Participants form six teams of their own choosing, with the instruction that no one is to be excluded. Once the teams are evenly sized, team members decide who will go first, second, and so on. The members of each team stand in a line behind their designated area (one line per hoop). The first person from each team should stand in the hoop in front of them. On the signal to go, the teams must find the pieces of paper that have negative traits written on them and must put them back into the paper bag. Teams will be timed on how long it takes them to place all the negative traits back in the bag. Once a piece of paper is unwrapped, it must be re-crumpled and placed in the bag, or discarded. Once the first round is over, the teacher or leader should challenge other teams to beat the previous time. At some point, the leader can take one person from each group to create a new team.

Here are some questions you might use for a discussion with your class or group:

- Why did it take so long for people to pick their own teams?
- Without giving names, how was the choice of who was on each team determined? How did you decide the order of players on your team?
- How did you feel when the leader decided to take one person from each team to create a new group, taking your choice of teams away?
- Was this a fair decision? Did it affect the effort you gave in this activity? If so, why?

Watch My Back

AGES: Middle school through high school

EQUIPMENT: Labels with words representing various emotions printed on them

PURPOSE: This activity is meant to help young people understand the emotions that may be triggered by particular events.

PROCEDURE: Before this activity begins, the class or group makes a list of a variety of words representing emotions (the list that follows contains suggestions). The teacher or group leader gives definitions and an example of an event that could trigger a particular emotion to ensure that participants understand each of the words. The teacher or leader then places an emotion label on each player's back (it's okay if there are duplicates of some emotions). Players move around the area and ask yes or no questions of other players to try to figure out which emotion label they are wearing. Only one question at a time may be asked. If a player guesses the correct emotion, the person he asked the question of takes the label off his back. The player who guessed correctly then places the label on the front of his shirt and continues the activity by answering questions for other players. The game ends when all players have successfully guessed their emotions.

Sample List of Emotions:

Anger	Frustration	Embarrassment
Fear	Confusion	Sadness
Disappointment	Loneliness	Happiness
Resentment	Paranoia	Surprise
Excitement	Pride	Helplessness
Guilt	Anxiety	Love
Alienation	Hostility	Discouragement
Confidence	Boredom	Humiliation
Jealousy	Depression	Remorse
Relief	Shame	

Adapted, by permission, from J.L. Skully, 2000, *The power of social skills in character development: Helping diverse learners succeed* (Port Chester, NY: Dude Publishing), 126.

Knotty Dilemma

AGES: Middle school through high school

EQUIPMENT: 1 jump rope (made with rope, approximately 6 feet [1.5 meters] long) per team of 4 to 6 players

PURPOSE: The purpose of this activity is to provide a cooperative problem-solving experience. Members of each team take turns to be the first team to untie a previously tied rope.

PROCEDURE: Team members sit in a small circle. One rope is given to each team. The teams must cooperatively tie a rope into multiple, loosely tied knots, making it difficult for another team to untie. The teacher or group leader decides the rotation order of the team members. On the signal to go, each team member is given 15 seconds to tie a knot, or multiple knots, in the rope.

Once everyone is given a chance to tie the rope, the ropes are redistributed to other teams. On the signal to go, each team member is given 15 seconds to untie the rope, until the rope is entirely untied. The first team to successfully untie the rope wins that round.

In round 2, players tie the ropes as in the previous round. Without giving prior notice, have each team keep their own rope and untie it. In round 3, when it's time to untie the ropes, announce that there are no special rules for how it must be untied.

Here are some suggestions for discussion questions:

- Was this a frustrating experience? If so, why?
- Did you think the second round, in which each team kept their own rope, was fair? Why or why not? (If you are a classroom teacher, this would be a good time to discuss student-student and student-teacher fairness.)
- Did the group work cooperatively and fairly? Did everyone get a fair turn, particularly when there were no specific rules as to who should untie the rope or in what order? Can you think of a better way to do this activity?

Carpet-Square Relays

AGES: Grade 4 through high school

EQUIPMENT: Carpet squares (2 for each person), and cones for marking start and finish areas

PURPOSE: This activity provides a cooperative experience that requires teamwork and control. Participants need to work together to keep their balance and move in unison on carpet squares.

PROCEDURE: The activity needs to be done on a hard, smooth surface such as a gym floor. Carpet squares should be placed carpet side down. This allows the carpet to travel freely, and the players' feet remain secure against the friction side of the carpet. Safety is of the utmost importance, so let the young people know that if their bodies fall to the ground, their team is disqualified. This will help keep them from sacrificing safety for speed.

Suggestions for various relays follow. Note that it's not a good idea to have more than six members on one team. More than that would allow for too much wait time and possible boredom or disruptive behavior.

Relay 1: Each team should consist of five or six members. The first member on each team must skate or slide with one carpet square under each foot around a designated cone and back. Once a turn is completed, that person should tag the next team member on the hand and proceed to the end of their line. If anyone's foot comes off of a square, he must immediately place the carpet under his foot and continue his turn. The first team to complete the task wins the round.

Relay 2: Try to complete the same course with two people attached at a time. One person holds onto the shoulders of the person in front.

Relay 3: Try to have the whole team maneuver the course, holding onto each others' shoulders.

Relay 4: This is a rescue relay. Teams can pretend that they are in a blizzard, and the carpets are snow shoes. One member of the team stands on opposite sides of the area, approximate 30 feet (9 meters) away from the rest of the team. On the signal to go, that team member must travel on the squares to rescue a teammate. That teammate must hold onto the rescuer's shoulders and travel with her back to the starting point. Then, the two teammates go back to pick up a third teammate and proceed in the same manner.

Relay 5: All teams should be close enough to each other so that the first member of each team can connect hands or elbows, making a new team. The team should travel together, on their own carpet squares, to a designated point (perhaps between two cones placed at the other side of the room). If any member of the team should lose her balance, she should call out, "Stop." The team should let go of hands and freeze. They hold hands again and resume movement as soon as all team members have regained their balance and have placed one foot on each of their carpet squares. The teacher or group leader should time each team's turn. The team that can accomplish this task the fastest wins the round. Once team one's turn is complete, the new front member of each line becomes team two and proceeds in the same manner.

Here are some questions for discussion that you might use with your group or class:

- What made this activity difficult?
- What did you like or dislike about this activity?
- Did you feel different about the other members of the class when people you had competed against were now on your team?

A Handshake to Remember

AGES: Grade 4 through high school

EQUIPMENT: None

PURPOSE: This activity gives young people an appropriate way to acknowledge and include each other as important members of the class or group.

PROCEDURE: Divide the class or group into teams of five or so. Ask each team to come up with a simple handshake, a unique way to greet each other. Instruct the team members to be sure to be polite and to look others in the eye as they acknowledge them. After each team has a handshake, bring the class or group together. Ask each team to share their handshakes with the rest of the group. After everyone has shared, ask each person to sit down in a place where there is enough space for someone to walk around them.

Show the group which handshake will begin the game. Choose one of the handshakes the teams have designed, if appropriate, or make up your own. The handshake should be subtle and not noticeably different from a regular handshake. Once the handshake is shown to the group, everyone closes their eyes. The teacher or group leader randomly taps five participants on the shoulder. Once participants are chosen, the leader asks everyone to open their eyes and asks a participant to demonstrate a typical handshake. The handshake should be firm, but not hard. Participants are instructed to stand up, walk around, and greet each other with handshakes. Only the designated participants will use the special, predetermined handshake. All others will use regular handshakes. The object of the game is to be the first player to go to the

teacher or leader and identify all of the designated participants. The designated participants are not permitted to identify other designated participants, because they have fewer people to identify.

While doing this activity, I noticed that many of my students were not accustomed to greeting each other with a proper handshake while looking each other in the eyes. One student squeezed too hard and then wondered why others didn't want to shake his hand. I discussed with the class that first impressions are very important and that when you greet someone, it's a way of showing respect and acknowledgement for someone else. You might want to have a similar discussion with your class or group.

Peace Starts With Me

AGES: Grade 4 and up

EQUIPMENT: A clothespin for each person, with one side reading "Conflict" and the other side reading "Peace"

PURPOSE: The purpose of this activity is to help young people realize that one person can make a difference and that many changes in the world have been the result the actions of one person.

PROCEDURE: The class or group should be scattered in a designated area—about the size of a volleyball court for a group of 30. Everyone in the group should place a clothespin on one of their sleeves, with the Conflict side facing up. The teacher or group leader asks one person to switch his clothespin to the Peace side. On the command to go, the Peace person needs to tag someone. No one should try to be tagged. Once a Conflict person is tagged, she switches her clothespin to the Peace side and helps her tagger convert others to Peace. The round is over when all group members have Peace on their sleeves.

Discuss with your class or group the ideas behind this activity: One person can make a difference. Peace can be spread, and it needs to start from within. Negative messages can be spread as well as positive messages. Harmful gossip and untruths can easily start with one person and spread to many others.

Make a list of worthwhile causes with your group. Have them think about injustices in the world and ways that those injustices might be resolved. Ask them how they think one person could make a difference.

Scorpion Tag

AGES: Grade 3 through middle school

EQUIPMENT: None

PURPOSE: In this activity, individuals work together, as either leaders or followers, to accomplish a task.

PROCEDURE: The game starts with one tagger for every 8 to 10 players. The object of the game is to acquire the longest line (tail). No one should try to get tagged in this game. If a player is tagged, she must hold onto the shoulders of the last person in the line of the person who tagged her. The line must travel together, staying attached. The only person who can tag others is the first person in the line. The tail, once it gets long enough, can wrap around and strategically hinder the progress of nontagged players. Once all players are tagged, the longest line of players wins that round.

It's important to discuss safety prior to this activity. Make the playing area small enough to prohibit fast, uncontrolled movement. Continue making the area smaller as more and more children are tagged. The attached lines need to be careful not to trip each other while running. It would be beneficial for attached runners to slightly stagger themselves, so legs will not collide. To encourage safety, make the rule that if anyone needs to disconnect, the tagger loses its tail and must start over again.

A variation on this game goes as follows: Once the tail has five people in it, the tail becomes a stinger. The last player can now tag others. The player does so by holding onto the person in front of him with one hand and using the other hand to tag.

You might use the following questions with your class or group after they have done the activity:

- Which variation of the activity did you like best? Why?
- What made this activity difficult?
- Was it frustrating for you? If so, why?
- If you were the tagger, how did you feel about being the lead person with others hanging on to you?
- If you weren't the leader, how did you feel about following?
- What was your team's strategy? Was it effective?
- Was communication difficult for you or your team?
- Was your team organized?

Take Me Home

AGES: Grade 4 and up

EQUIPMENT: 2 cones for each team

PURPOSE: To create an environment that requires responsibility and trust while team members complete a team task.

PROCEDURE: Discuss with the class or group what it means to trust others. Ask them if they are responsible enough for others to trust in them.

Divide the group into teams of about six participants each. One cone should be at the starting line for each team and the second cone should be about 45 feet (13.5 meters) away. The first person on each team should stand at the starting cone. On the signal to go, the first person should run or walk fast around the cone in front of her. Once around the cone and back to the start, she should tag the next player in her line. The tagged player should close his eyes and hang onto the shoulders of the person in front of him. Once they proceed around the cone in front of them, the lead person should tag the next person in line. The tagged person is the new sighted leader. Previously tagged players should close their eyes and hold on to the new leader. If anyone on the team should disconnect, the team must reconnect and count to 30. The first team to bring all blind players around the cone and back to the starting point wins that round.

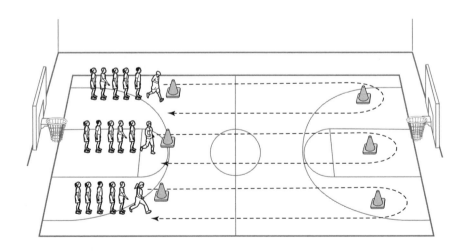

You might want to try a second round with obstacles in the way. Players need to be responsible and watch out for the safety of the nonsighted players. Another alternative would be for each team to race around obstacles in pairs. The "blind" person would be in the front with the sighted person holding onto her shoulders and leading from behind. The blind person should have his arms out in front of him and bent at the elbows. The arms will act as bumpers and help keep the children safe. Once the pairs have completed their turns, they would go to the ends of their own lines.

Here are questions you might ask the group after they've finished the activity:

- Was it easier to lead the team or to be a follower? Why?
- What made this activity difficult?
- What did you like about this activity?
- What didn't you like about this activity?
- Did it simulate real life in any way?

Developing Self-Esteem

O ur skills, talents, and ability to interact with the outside world play a part in determining how strongly we value and respect ourselves. Self-esteem is a measure of our self-worth (both physical and emotional), self-respect, and personal potential. Many people think that a positive self-image is important, but few know how to achieve it. Without self-esteem, it is more difficult to overcome adversities, control our emotions, and deal effectively with others.

A young person's ability to stand up to peer pressure is greatly influenced by his or her self-esteem level. Children who have poor self-concepts will more readily let others make important decisions for them, because their need for peer acceptance is greater than their ability to make healthy choices. Those with higher self-esteem have confidence and control over their own lives and tend to make better decisions.

Wanting to fit in and belong is a natural part of growing up. If the desire to fit in is *too* strong, though, kids may let pressure from friends influence them to turn to alcohol, tobacco, or illegal drugs. Marketing campaigns may also act as a source of pressure. According to a 1990 Scholastic/CNN survey, 56 percent of students in grades 5 through 12 said that alcohol advertising encourages them to drink.

In order to avoid dangerous behavior and putting your health at risk, certain skills are necessary. Refusal skills are very important. The ability to say no and mean it is essential for avoiding peer pressure. Kids should know ahead of time what they are willing and not willing to do. They should practice saying no and resisting peer pressure in difficult situations; when the actual problem arises, it will be easier for them to handle.

Everyone experiences frustration, joy, failure, and success during the process of learning. While learning to cope with the demands of life, young people need to feel successful. Having resiliency skills can help them successfully overcome the obstacles and setbacks that inevitably occur. Research-based resiliency builders (Henderson, 2002) include relationships, humor, inner direction, perceptiveness, independence, a positive view of personal future, flexibility, love of learning, self-motivation, competence, self-worth, spirituality, perseverance, and creativity.

The activities in this chapter emphasize self-esteem, personal attributes, values, self-awareness, and the effects people have on others. By gaining a better sense of who they are, young people can learn ways to change and control destructive or inappropriate behaviors.

Visualization (A Way to Build Self-Esteem)

AGES: Middle school through high school

EQUIPMENT: None

PURPOSE: This activity helps young people develop self-awareness and confidence in their ability to achieve particular tasks, and it can be used to enhance self-esteem. After learning a basic technique such as the one presented here, young people can go on to use visualization to picture themselves being successful in situations that previously had completely intimidated them. Having young people picture themselves overcoming obstacles or being successful in difficult situations can increase their confidence in real-life situations.

I've noticed great improvement in the behavior of the students in my classes after they do this activity. The visualization activity has been a calming experience for those of my students who have trouble relaxing.

PROCEDURE: Lead your group through this activity by using the following script, which you can record in advance and play for the group if you wish. Be sure to explain and demonstrate diaphragmatic breathing for participants before beginning the activity.

"Find a comfortable place. Close your eyes, and take a slow, deep breath. Exhale slowly. Breathe in slowly, from the diaphragm; exhale slowly. Do this several times; in, out; in, out. Think about a safe place that you enjoy visiting. Concentrate on what you see. Try to block out all sounds. Focus on the details of what you see. You are a passive observer. Continue to breathe in and out slowly. Enjoy the scenery. It might be something in nature or the people you see. Now try to think about the sounds that you hear. It might be the sound of the waves or children's laughter. Concentrate on the sounds that you hear. What kinds of smells are there? Is it the smell of a barbecue, freshly baked cookies, or the salt-filled air at the beach? Concentrate on the smell. What tastes are you experiencing? Is it the taste of your favorite food? Is the food sweet or sour? What do you feel at this special place? Is it the feel of the hot sand on the bottom of your feet or the wind hitting your face? Is it softness of your cat's fur? Think about the different things that you touch. Realize that you can visit this place often. This is a place where you can go to relax. Now come back to the room here. Become aware of your breathing. When you're ready, open your eyes."

A variation on this activity is to have people visualize a single object, such as an apple. Instruct them to visualize the apple's color and shape and to imagine the feel of it, the taste of it, and the sound of the crunching, concentrating on one detail at a time.

See Three (Visual Acuity Activity)

AGES: All ages

EQUIPMENT: 3 clothespins

PURPOSE: This activity helps participants notice details and become more aware of their surroundings. It also forces students to become aware of their peripheral vision while walking in a forward direction, which broadens their line of sight.

PROCEDURE: Participants should sit down in a scattered formation. There should be enough room for a person to walk between participants. Once seated, participants close their eyes and hold one hand open behind their backs. The leader gives the clothespins to three people. Participants who receive a clothespin open their eyes and place it somewhere on their bodies, with a little bit of it showing (the clothespin should not be placed in an embarrassing spot). Once all clothespins have been placed, the rest of the participants open their eyes.

Everyone is asked to stand up and walk around in an area about the size of half a basketball court. Participants should act normal. Instruct them to keep walking and not to stare or appear to be stalking any other participant. No one is to speak or make gestures (no pointing). Those who are wearing the clothespins should never sit down. Those without the clothespins, once they've spotted all three people wearing them, quietly go and sit down outside of the playing area, not telling anyone else what they've seen. Stop the activity when there are a few participants still looking for the clothespins, so that

you don't get down to just one person who hasn't been able to spot the clothespins.

As a twist to this activity, I will often wear one of the clothespins. Most students assume that the teacher is not involved in the activity. Some students have said that I deceived them. I tell them that I never said I wasn't participating in the activity. This is a good lesson on staying focused and not making assumptions.

Mystery Tag (Visual Awareness)

AGES: All ages

EQUIPMENT: None

PURPOSE: This activity heightens participants' sense of sight. Being able to quickly scan a group for unusual behavior can make you more aware of your surroundings. The ability to sense danger before it strikes may help participants avoid dangerous situations in real life.

PROCEDURE: Before starting this activity, you may want to discuss ways to avoid dangerous situations and how to seek help if necessary. I tell my students a story about when I was younger and my car broke down. I was in the car with three other girls and it was late at night. I saw a car zoom by in the opposite direction and then make an abrupt U-turn about 100 yards (30 meters) down the street from us. A man in this same car approached us to ask us if we wanted help. He said that it was no problem and that he was going the same direction anyway. Because I was observant, I knew that wasn't true. I had already alerted my friends about this vehicle and the U-turn. We told the man thanks but that we already had help on the way. He may have been a Good Samaritan, but we were not going to take a chance.

This activity begins with all participants sitting in a scattered formation, with room to walk between and around each person. When participants' eyes are closed, the group leader picks two people to be secret taggers. The group leader may also act as one of the taggers but must be very discrete.

While nontaggers are randomly walking in a small area (approximately half the size of a basketball court), the taggers discretely try to tag other players. All players must keep moving. They are not allowed to stop and stare. If a tagger is tagged by another tagger, or is touched by anyone, he should ignore the tag and continue to move. If players are tagged or touched by anyone, they must go and sit down after counting silently to five (this makes it less obvious to others who tagged the players). There is no talking allowed during this game, even when a player has been tagged. Nontaggers should avoid making contact with other players. As more people are tagged, make the playing area smaller. This will make it less obvious who the tagger is and it won't prolong the activity.

Some possible discussion questions are:

- Did you notice anything unusual about the tagger's behavior?
- Did your behavior change knowing that a tagger was nearby?
- Was it hard for you to act normal?
- If you knew who the taggers were, what did you do to try to stay safe?

Hear Me, Hear Me (Sensory Acuity)

AGES: All ages

EQUIPMENT: None

PURPOSE: This activity is intended to heighten participants' sense of hearing. Because they concentrate on only one sense in this activity, it's easier for people to stay focused and ignore unnecessary distractions. When people are more attuned to the sounds around them, they may more easily perceive that danger is approaching or that someone nearby is in distress and needs help.

PROCEDURE: Participants sit with their eyes closed in a scattered formation, 3 to 5 feet (1 to 1.5 meters) apart. Participants should focus their attention on sounds in the area. The object of this activity is for participants to turn

their bodies, with eyes closed, and face the direction of the noise that they hear. Instruct them never to allow the noise to be at their backs. The group leader walks around to see how aware people are of others around them. If a participant doesn't react to the subtle noise of the leader's walking, the leader may need to make more obvious noises such as coughing, snapping fingers, clapping, and so forth.

To add a little confusion to the activity, I sometimes tap participants on the shoulder and have them walk around with me. It's funny to see the perplexed expressions when the seated participants hear noises coming from multiple directions.

Challenge other people to see if they can quietly walk among the seated participants without being heard. Another way of doing this activity would be to have one person seated in the middle of the room, with eyes closed. All other participants should be seated along the four walls, or in a square formation. The leader points to a participant, and that person must try to tap the person in the center of the room on the shoulder—without being heard. If the player with eyes closed hears the participant approaching, she points in his direction without opening her eyes. If she points directly at the moving participant, that participant's turn is over, and he sits down and freezes at that spot. The participant with closed eyes trades places with anyone who is able to tap her on the shoulder before being identified. If the tagger does not wish to have a turn in the middle, he can choose someone else to take his place.

Pride Is the Prize

AGES: Grade 4 through high school

EQUIPMENT: None

PURPOSE: In this activity, young people think about the accomplishments that have made them happy, regardless of the reward, thereby becoming familiar with the concept of intrinsic motivation.

PROCEDURE: Have participants make a list of physical accomplishments they were not rewarded for but which they are proud of, and then have a group discussion about the items listed. You might want to ask the group these questions:

- What does pride feel like?
- How do you develop pride?

Whenever students ask me what they'll get if they accomplish a particular task, my answer is usually "pride." I tell them that pride is the best gift of all. Pride can last longer than any monetary gift or material object.

I've heard professional athletes say that their greatest sports experience was when they were younger and participated in the sport for pure enjoyment. It's often their college days that bring the fondest memories—a time before they received their big bonuses and high salaries; before the rewards that turned their love of sport into a job.

When I ask students to think about accomplishments that made them proud even though no one noticed, many are hard pressed to come up with any ideas. One student told me that there's nothing she's done for which her parents haven't recognized her.

I believe that as teachers and youth-group leaders, it's our responsibility to help young people see that they can develop pride by doing things because they feel good doing them, rather than because they'll be rewarded in some way.

The Power of Suggestion

AGES: Middle school through high school

EQUIPMENT: None

PURPOSE: This activity shows young people that self-talk has powerful effects on behavior (both positive and negative) and it can be a way for them to validate their actions and themselves.

PROCEDURE: Read the following information to your class or group and have a discussion about it.

In the book *First Class Character Education: Activities Program* (Koehler, 2001), an experiment was conducted to demonstrate the power of self-talk. A person held his arms out in front of him, parallel to the ground, and said, "I am a bad person" 10 times out loud. After he had done that, another person tried to pull his arms down to his sides while he resisted. Then, the same person held out his arms again, only this time he said, "I am a good person" 10 times out loud. And again the other person tried to pull his arms down. After the speaker had repeated the positive phrase ("I am a good person") 10 times, it was much harder for the other person to lower his arms.

You might use the following question with your class or group as a means of elaborating on the concept of positive versus negative self-talk.

> Why do you think it was so much easier for the other person to pull the speaker's arms down after he had repeated the positive phrase than it was after he had repeated the negative one?

Ask the group for examples of each type of self-talk and discuss how it can hurt or help them.

Who Am I?

AGES: Grade 4 through high school

EQUIPMENT: Paper and writing implements

PURPOSE: In this activity, participants think about what makes them unique and special, sharing personal stories and listening to the stories of others. Acknowledging and accepting differences helps provide a healthy learning environment where everyone feels valued.

PROCEDURE: Have students or group members write down two facts and one lie about themselves. Choose participants to read their three statements out loud to the group. The participant should reread one statement at a time and let the group raise their hand if they think the statement read is a lie. Count the hands read for each statement to see if the majority of the group guessed correctly.

When you're finished with the preceding, ask each participant to state one fact about him- or herself out loud. After each participant states the fact, ask the rest of the group members to raise their hands if the same fact is true about them.

Remember Me

AGES: Grade 4 through high school

EQUIPMENT: None

PURPOSE: In this activity, young people think about their values and life goals.

PROCEDURE: Discuss the meaning of the words *reputation* and *character.* Then ask the group the following questions:

- What would you like to be known for (that is, what is one of your goals in life)?
- How will you prepare to reach that goal (that is, what character traits are necessary)?

Here's a way to talk about goals with your group:

Once we commit to our goals, it's important to know the steps to success. Goals that don't rely on the actions of others are much more feasible to accomplish. For instance, having a goal such as "I want to be known as the fastest sprinter in the world" is tricky, because it depends on many variables that are beyond your control: talent, timing, financial assistance, family support, and luck, to name some of them. Think about things you can control and behaviors you may need to change to reach your goals.

How Stressed Are You?

AGES: Grade 4 through middle school

EQUIPMENT: Copies of handout and writing implements

PURPOSE: This activity helps students understand how stress builds up and affects them and others around them. It also encourages them to come up with ways to relieve stress in their lives.

PROCEDURE: Copy the "Stress Test: How Stressed Are You?" handout included and distribute it to your students. Have them answer each statement by checking whether it applies to them regularly, sometimes, or rarely. Once they're done they can total their scores. Each answer of "Regularly" receives 3 points, each answer of "Sometimes" receives 2 points, and each answer of "Rarely" receives 1 point. The higher the score, the more stressed they are. After they've determined their score, have them write down ways to reduce their stress level.

Afterwards, as a group, you may have a discussion in which participants discuss their answers. Students may find they're not the only ones experiencing stress or that they are creating stress in others.

Stress Test: How Stressed Are You?

For each statement, select the response that most applies to you, then total your points and see where you are on the stress scale.
(Regularly = 3 pts. Sometimes = 2 pts. Rarely = 1 pt.)

	Regularly	Sometimes	Rarely
1. Minor problems get blown out of proportion, making you feel angry.	____	____	____
2. You eat when you aren't hungry because you're bored or distressed in some way.	____	____	____
3. It's hard for you to sit still.	____	____	____
4. It takes a long time for you to get to sleep because your mind thinks of too many things.	____	____	____
5. You feel you always have to be doing something.	____	____	____
6. Your schoolwork is suffering.	____	____	____
7. It's hard to make decisions or set priorities.	____	____	____
8. You often get head, back, or neck aches.	____	____	____
9. There's been an increase in the number of colds or flu you get.	____	____	____
10. You never think you're good enough.	____	____	____
11. You don't believe your friends when they tell you that you did a good job.	____	____	____

(continued)

From *Character-Building Activities: Teaching Responsibility, Interaction, and Group Dynamics* by Judy Demers, 2008, Champaign, IL: Human Kinetics.

(continued)

	Regularly	**Sometimes**	**Rarely**
12. You're always feeling rushed, or like there's not enough time to get things done.	____	____	____
13. You always feel like there's too much to do.	____	____	____
14. You often feel irritable or moody without knowing the reason why.	____	____	____
15. It's difficult for you to solve problems by breaking them into smaller pieces.	____	____	____
16. You often under- or overeat.	____	____	____
17. It's hard for you to laugh at yourself in a non-demeaning way.	____	____	____

TOTAL SCORE: _____ (Circle your total on the scale below.)

1 2 3 4 5 6 7 8 9 10 11 12 13 14 15 16 17 18 19 20 21 22 23 24 25 26 27 28 29 30 31 32+
unstressed   stressed

If you scored high on the scale, think of things you could do to lower your stress level.

_____

_____

_____

_____

_____

_____

From *Character-Building Activities: Teaching Responsibility, Interaction, and Group Dynamics* by Judy Demers, 2008, Champaign, IL: Human Kinetics.

How Tolerant Are You?

AGES: Grade 4 through middle school

EQUIPMENT: Copies of the handout and writing implements

PURPOSE: This assignment encourages young people to assess their levels of tolerance and self-control. By answering the questions, participants can get an idea of how they manage anger in various situations. Then they are asked to think about ways of becoming less angry and more tolerant.

PROCEDURE: Distribute copies of the handout to your group. Instruct participants to answer the questions on the handout to see how prone to either tolerance or anger they are. Ask those who find that they're more prone to anger to write down ways they think they could change their behavior. Then have participants think of other situations that make them angry, and discuss with them various positive ways of handling those situations.

How Tolerant Are You?

Read each of the 10 numbered statements, then circle the answer that best describes how you would usually react in each situation. When you're finished, count how many statements you circled answer *b* for, and give yourself 1 point for each. Next, circle the number that represents your total points at the bottom of the page. This will give you an idea of how tolerant or angry you tend to be in certain situations.

1. Your little sister is being noisy while you are trying to study.
   a. You calmly ask her to play somewhere else.
   b. You are offended and immediately start yelling at her.

2. Your friend is talking about you behind your back.
   a. You tell him that this hurts your feelings and that you want to find out why it's happening.
   b. You are very angry, and you start talking about him to others.

3. Your brother or sister spills something on clothing that he or she borrowed from you.
   a. You calmly discuss with your sibling how it will be taken care of.
   b. In a rage, you run into your sibling's room to grab the first thing that you can find.

(continued)

From *Character-Building Activities: Teaching Responsibility, Interaction, and Group Dynamics* by Judy Demers, 2008, Champaign, IL: Human Kinetics.

(continued)

4. You're in a long line at the video store.
   a. You mentally make plans for the rest of your day while you are waiting.
   b. You become impatient and wish the clerks would move a little faster.

5. A team member tells you how you could have scored in a soccer game.
   a. You listen to the advice and think about whether or not it makes sense.
   b. You think of it as a personal attack and criticize the way that person played.

6. Daily life is filled with minor annoyances.
   a. You agree with this statement, but you realize that most annoyances can be overcome.
   b. You agree with this statement, and you feel that annoyances make life very difficult.

7. You're in the middle of a stressful situation, and you're trying to control yourself.
   a. You see how controlling your anger stops you from over-reacting.
   b. You can't think straight; the situation makes you so angry that you just explode.

8. Someone doesn't agree with you.
   a. You try to convince her, but you also know that the person is allowed to have her own opinion.
   b. You become agitated, and you harass the person until she changes her mind.

9. Someone laughs at you.
   a. You realize that what you did was funny, and you laugh, too.
   b. You feel offended, and you verbally attack the person.

10. Someone bumps into you in a crowded room.
    a. You assume it was a mistake, and if the person apologizes, you accept the apology.
    b. You push the person back; after all, he should get what he deserves.

From *Character-Building Activities: Teaching Responsibility, Interaction, and Group Dynamics* by Judy Demers, 2008, Champaign, IL: Human Kinetics.

Total number of *b* answers:_____

Circle the total number of questions that you answered *b* to:

Tolerant   1   2   3   4   5   6   7   8   9   10   Angry

If your score was 6 or higher, meaning you react with anger more often than with tolerance, think about how you might become more tolerant and lower your score.

_____

_____

_____

_____

_____

_____

From *Character-Building Activities: Teaching Responsibility, Interaction, and Group Dynamics* by Judy Demers, 2008, Champaign, IL: Human Kinetics.

Mixed Emotions

AGES: Grade 4 through middle school

EQUIPMENT: Paper and writing implements

PURPOSE: This activity helps young people realize that everyone experiences emotions in different ways and that they can't predict what effect words and situations may have on others. The activity also helps participants to become aware of their emotions and understand how emotions can affect their own behavior and that of others.

PROCEDURE: Copy the story listed in this activity and distribute it to your participants. Have them complete the story by filling in the blanks, using the following words: *embarrassed, afraid, happy, sad, confident,* and *worried.*

You might ask the participants to share their own stories involving the emotions mentioned in the preceding story ("Have you ever felt any of the emotions that the person in the story did? What was the situation?"). Not everyone reacts to situations in the same way, of course; keep that in mind when participants are sharing. Then ask your young people to write true stories of their own about a situation in which they felt mixed emotions. This is a good way for participants to communicate on a personal level. In my classes, I use the following personal story as an example; you might share one of your own with your class or group.

One of the most memorable moments in which I was filled with mixed emotions occurred on my first day of student teaching. I was young, naïve, and ready to change the world. I was teaching beginning swimmers. I was in the best shape of my life (I was trying to make the Olympic team for middle-distance running). My supervising teacher received a phone call, so she left the pool deck for what seemed like forever.

She had me do what I felt was a ridiculous warm-up. The students were to run around the shallow end, one behind the other. There was no rope separating the shallow end from the deep end. By running that way, the students created a whirlpool action, and the current carried some students into the deep water. Several students pretended to be drowning and then popped back up. Four or five girls were standing on the deck, and they were laughing at the girls bobbing up and down. Finally, one student ran around the side of the pool and screamed at me, "She's really drowning!" At first I didn't believe it, because the girls on the deck nearby continued to laugh. I saw one girl go down and not come back up. I knew I had to do something.

At first, I did all the wrong things. I took off my new watch (I don't know why), and I kept on my heavy shoes and the whistle around my neck. I jumped in after her. I struggled with the girl, who immediately grabbed my whistle and hung on for dear life. I was tiring quickly, and I couldn't breathe. I took the girl down to the bottom of the pool, kicked off of the bottom, and thrust

72

her toward the surface. I was terrified. I thought I was going to die, but I had to save her (I did manage to save the girl). As I reached the surface, gasping for air, I saw the same girls on the deck—they were within reach of us. Were they going to watch us both die?

I still remember my emotions on that day. I was distressed that my supervising teacher had left us alone for such a long time. My first concern was the drowning student, and I was terrified at the thought that she might die. I was also afraid for my life. In addition, I have never been so angry as I was with the girls nearby on the deck (afterward, they said that they hadn't known what to do and hadn't thought they were good enough swimmers to help us). Several members of the class told me that I was brave and that I was a hero, but I didn't feel that way. I felt embarrassed that I had let my supervising teacher down and disgusted with myself for doing the wrong things. I threw my custom-made track shoes in the garbage can and went home barefoot that day.

The soccer championships were being held the next day. My best friend

was hurt so he/she couldn't play. That made me very _____.

I was _____ about the game and couldn't sleep the night

before. I was _____ that I would cause the team to lose.

The day of the tournament, while I was running for the ball during

a game, I tripped on my laces. I was so _____. People

in the stands started calling out words of encouragement. That made

me _____. I regained my composure and started to feel

more _____. I ended up scoring the winning goal!

From *Character-Building Activities: Teaching Responsibility, Interaction, and Group Dynamics* by Judy Demers, 2008, Champaign, IL: Human Kinetics.

Consequences

AGES: Middle school through high school

EQUIPMENT: Copies of the handout and writing implements

PURPOSE: This activity is intended to help young people realize that emotions do not occur in isolation—that is, that the things we do have consequences and may result in our feeling certain emotions.

PROCEDURE: Distribute the "Behavior-Consequence-Feeling" chart to your group. As a lead-in to the activity, ask the following questions and discuss the answers with the group.

Do you think about consequences before you act? If you ever have doubts about whether or not to do something, think about these things:

- How do you think engaging in this behavior will affect you?
- How do you think engaging in the behavior will affect those around you (your friends, teachers, coaches)?
- Think of the people you deeply care about, and visualize the expressions on their faces when they find out about the behavior. Will it make them proud? Will they be disappointed or lose respect for you?
- If you think the behavior might affect you and those around you in a negative way, is it worth the risk?

After you've discussed behaviors and the resulting consequences and emotions with the group, ask them to complete the chart, listing possible behaviors and consequences that might be associated with the listed feelings.

Here is a discussion point you might use in talking about this activity with your class or group:

> Looking at a particular consequence and feeling, and thinking backward to the behaviors that may have caused them, can give us insights about what we want to do in the future. Thinking ahead to consequences and the feelings we might have if we engage in certain behaviors can help us make better choices. For example, if a friend is pressuring you to smoke (behavior), thinking about the trouble you would be in with your parents (consequence) and the sadness (feeling) you would feel about disappointing them might make it easier to say no.

Behavior	Consequence	Feeling
		Nervous
		Confident
		Happy
		Sad
		Angry
		Satisfied
		Frustrated
		Proud
		Smart
		Accepted
		Disappointed
		Horrible
		Safe
		Relaxed
		Important
		Bored
		Respected

From *Character-Building Activities: Teaching Responsibility, Interaction, and Group Dynamics* by Judy Demers, 2008, Champaign, IL: Human Kinetics.

Self-Praise Versus Arrogance

AGES: Middle school through high school

EQUIPMENT: Copies of the handout and writing implements

PURPOSE: This activity helps build self-esteem by teaching young people how to acknowledge what they do well without being arrogant.

PROCEDURE: Distribute the "Self-Talk or Arrogance?" handout and ask participants to fill it out. When they've finished, you might use the following as discussion points.

Here are some talking points and follow-up questions you might use with your group as you discuss their answers on the handout:

- Self-praise and encouragement are necessary for becoming self-motivated.
- Positive self-talk is different from bragging and saying that you're better than someone else.
- When you compare yourself to others, nothing is definite.
- You can't control what other people are going to do or how they're going to feel during a particular activity.
- Why might it be unhealthy to try to build yourself up by putting someone else down?
- What are some possible consequences of showing arrogant behavior?

Self-Talk or Arrogance?

Decide whether each statement is positive self-talk or arrogance and place a check mark on the line in the appropriate column.

	Positive self-talk	Arrogance
I did well on my skills test today.	_____	_____
I studied hard for the test and felt prepared.	_____	_____
I ran the 440 faster than last time.	_____	_____
I did more push-ups than everyone else.	_____	_____
Stretching every day is making me more flexible.	_____	_____
Training hard has made me more fit.	_____	_____
Training hard has made me unbeatable.	_____	_____

From *Character-Building Activities: Teaching Responsibility, Interaction, and Group Dynamics* by Judy Demers, 2008, Champaign, IL: Human Kinetics.

What Do You Value Most?

AGES: All ages

EQUIPMENT: None

PURPOSE: This activity asks students to think about what they value, and it exposes them to the concept of individual differences—they may find that the things they consider valuable are not the same things that others place value on. Depending on the ages of the participants, you may need to clarify the difference between monetary and emotional value before doing this exercise. And you also might want to point out the difference between replaceable and irreplaceable things.

PROCEDURE: Present the following scenario to your group (verbally):

There is an emergency, and you must leave your house in 5 minutes. You are allowed to take only what you can carry. What would you take with you, and why?

Allow each participant time to share with the rest of the group.

Character Scramble

AGES: Middle through high school

EQUIPMENT: Character trait cards, trait labels, and cut-out letters forming the word *character*

PURPOSE: In this activity, young people identify positive character traits and apply them to real-life situations.

PROCEDURE: The teacher or group leader should first emphasize that no put-downs should occur at any time, and participants should not be pressured to share personal or embarrassing stories.

Participants get into groups of four or five people. Each group is given a card with a list of character traits and definitions on it (see the following list for possible character traits to include). The participants in each group discuss the traits among themselves and come up with examples of real-life situations in which the traits are displayed. If no one in the group can come up with an example of a particular trait, the group develops a short skit to act it out.

Character Traits

Honesty: Being sincere and truthful, having integrity

Respect: Honoring others and their rights

Courage: Being brave; being confident to try new things

Self-control: Controlling behavior despite one's feelings

Justness: Obeying rules; standing up for one's own rights and the rights of others

Humility: Being modest; being willing to accept correction and learn from one's mistakes

Responsibility: Being accountable for oneself, or for the welfare of another

Kindness: Being tender, considerate, friendly

Determination: Being motivated to reach a goal

Meanwhile, nine "trait stations" are set up around the area where the groups are working. Each station is supplied with cut-out letters (one of the letters in the word *character,* so that one station has all C's, another all H's, another all A's, and so forth. The number of cut-out letters at each station needs to match the number of small groups you have, so that the leader can award a letter to each group. Assign one leader to each station; the leaders wear a label with one of the character traits printed on it.

Once a group is ready, its members travel together to each trait station (only one group can be at a station at a time). When a group reaches a station, its members must give the leader a real-life example of that station's trait, or perform a short skit. If the trait is accurately represented, the leader gives the group a letter (leaders can give suggestions to groups that are having trouble). Once all of the groups have letters from all of the character trait stations, the participants in each group must figure out what word the letters form (*character*). Each group works as an individual unit to decipher the word.

Once all the groups have discovered the word, the class or group as a whole shares their experiences. Ask for volunteers to show skits or give examples for each of the character traits.

Choose to Be Enthused

AGES: Grade 4 through high school

EQUIPMENT: None

PURPOSE: This activity is intended to help young people become aware of their self-talk and to have them work on changing any negative self-talk they identify to something positive.

PROCEDURE: Ask participants to carry a small journal with them during the day. When they are able, they should write down their positive and negative self-talk as the day progresses. Ask the participant to read the journal at the end of the day. Ask how the number of negative comments compared with the number of positive comments.

Once participants have entered comments in their journals for several days, ask them to think about what their attitude typically is when they wake up in the morning, and point out that that attitude might affect the course of their whole day. Then introduce the concept of positive self-talk, in the form of affirmations. You might share these sample affirmations with participants, as examples:

Today is a new day!

I can't always be in control of what happens to me, but I have some choice about how I will react to various circumstances.

I can choose my attitude.

I am resilient.

I have something good to offer.

I am smart.

Are You Superstitious?

AGES: Grade 4 through high school

EQUIPMENT: None

PURPOSE: This activity encourages young people to think about their habits and superstitions and what the basis for them might be.

PROCEDURE: Ask your class or group to think about the following: Before a sporting event or a challenge of any kind (a big test in school, for instance), is there any particular ritual that you perform? (You might use the example of wearing a "lucky" pair of socks.) Let everyone who has such a ritual explain it to the group.

After everyone has shared, you might use these questions for further discussion:

- Why do you think people rely on superstition? Are they afraid of failure? Do they feel their superstition gives them an advantage?
- Can superstitions be harmful? If yes, in what ways?
- Are superstitions passed down through the generations? Can you give an example from your own life?

Share Your Family Traditions

AGES: Grade 3 and up

EQUIPMENT: None

PURPOSE: Family traditions are often passed down from generation to generation. In this activity, participants are given opportunities to share and to listen to stories about others' traditions. Experiences of family, friendship, and love may be expressed in different ways, but they are important to all of us.

PROCEDURE: Allow participants to share their family traditions with the group. This is a great way for children to get to know each other on a more personal level. Encourage them to ask questions of each other about the various traditions and cultures that are represented in the group.

Discuss with your group that it is important to be respectful and not critical when others share their personal stories. Explain to them that the more we can learn from and work with each other, the stronger we all can become.

Pride and Purpose

AGES: Grade 4 and up

EQUIPMENT: None

PURPOSE: This activity allows young people a chance to communicate personal information in a fun, nonthreatening way. When we have an opportunity to tell others what makes us proud, it helps us to focus our attention on the things that truly matter to us.

PROCEDURE:

> **Activity 1:**   Ask class or group members to find partners. Partners take turns acting out the following for each other:
> - What are you most proud of about yourself?
> - What are you most proud of about your family?
> - What are you most proud of about your school?
> - What are you most proud of about your community?
>
> **Activity 2:**   Partners take turns describing (using words this time) an object or a physical activity that they like to each other. Instruct them to give details but not to name the activities or objects in their descriptions.

After all of the partners share the information with each other, ask for volunteers who would like to share in front of the class.

I'm always amazed by what I learn about my students during this activity. And if the teacher takes part and shares the same information with her students, this becomes a good opportunity for the students to learn about their teacher as well.

Don't Cross the Line

AGES: Grade 4 and up

EQUIPMENT: None

PURPOSE: In this activity, young people have an opportunity to think about their personal boundaries and to practice assertiveness skills.

PROCEDURE: Have participants make a list of things that they would never do. Then ask them to answer the following questions.

- How do you effectively tell someone no?
- Are there ways of telling someone no and still being friends with that person?
- Are there times where you may not want to remain friends with a person?
- Do your friends honor your boundary lines?

While you're discussing the preceding questions with your class or group, you might want to offer these suggestions: It takes practice to get good at saying no. When you're at home, look in the mirror and practice saying no. Or practice role-playing with friends or family, inventing various scenarios in which you would have to say no. Be assertive, but not physical. Look the other person in the eyes and show them that you mean what you say. If you look away, giggle, or smile, or appear to be fidgety or nervous, your own mother won't believe you. If you give an excuse when you say no, be sure the excuse is one that gets you out of the situation for good. You don't want a person to pester you day after day. An example might be "No, I don't want to die young" when someone offers you a cigarette. That's an answer that won't logically allow them to ask you again. If the other person won't back down, you may need to walk away.

The Art of Compromise

AGES: Middle school through high school

EQUIPMENT: None

PURPOSE: Peaceful solutions to conflict often require compromise. In this activity, young people have an opportunity to think about what compromise entails and how and when it should be employed.

PROCEDURE: Ask your class or group to answer the following questions:

- What does compromise mean?
- When someone is willing to compromise, does it mean that he is weak or gives in?
- Do government leaders need to compromise?
- Describe a time when you were able to compromise to keep the peace.
- Is there ever a time when you shouldn't compromise? Give examples.

Sports Predicament

AGES: Middle school through high school (could be adapted for younger people by adding discussion and simplifying scenarios)

EQUIPMENT: None

PURPOSE: The purpose of this activity is to help young people develop appropriate strategies to deal with adverse behavior or conditions. Participants are given the opportunity to share personal opinions dealing with character development.

PROCEDURE: To begin the activity, one participant is asked to leave the room (or area) so that she can't hear what the group is saying. While the person is gone, the class discusses a predicament that has a physical element to it. When the person returns, she is allowed to ask five other participants what they would do in this situation. The participants she calls on have the right to pass if they don't have a good solution. Otherwise, participants should give helpful, productive hints without using specific terminology that would give the scenario away. A nonphysical example might be: You are in a car and the car stalls on the railroad tracks. A possible answer to "What would you do?" might be to open the door, get out, and run (rather than "I would yell at the train engineer to stop"). When the five questions have been answered, the participant who had left the room has a chance to guess what the situation was.

Once a scenario is guessed, and before you begin another round, you might encourage further discussion about positive and negative character traits regarding that particular situation.

Here are some sample scenarios you might use in your classes or groups. If participants prefer, give them the opportunity to make up their own scenarios.

1. Your best friend falls in the mud while going for the ball. The whole class starts to laugh at him. What would you do?

2. One of the weakest players in the class tries to join your team. No one wants her to join, and others on the team tell that person to go somewhere else. What would you do?

3. Someone on your volleyball team is afraid of the ball. Everyone starts putting that person down. What would you do?

4. You are the captain picking your team. You really want to win the tournament. Your best friend is not very skilled, but he wants to be on your team. What would you do?

5. Your coach asks you to intentionally hurt one of the key soccer players on the opposite team. What would you do?

6. In football practice, you see several of the larger players ganging up on one of the weaker players. What would you do?

7. The night before a big tournament, your friends want you to stay out late and party. They tell you everyone is going and it won't hurt you. What would you do?

8. No one wants to work with, or include, the special needs student in the class. What would you do?

9. The captain of the football team, one of the most popular students at school, offers you a cigarette. What would you do?

Give and Take

AGES: Middle school through high school

EQUIPMENT: Five cones and one blindfold per team

PURPOSE: This activity gives young people the opportunity both to follow a leader and to help lead others. They will be exposed to distractions and limitations that could affect their performance. The hope is that by participating in and later discussing the activity, participants might become more sympathetic to the learning disabilities and needs of others.

PROCEDURE: Divide the class or group into teams, preferably with the same number on each (six to a team is a good number). Split each team in half, so that half of the team is in a line facing the other half of the team in a line (approximately 30 feet [9 meters] apart). Five cones are randomly placed between each team. The start side should be the same for each team. The start person for each team should be blindfolded.

On the command to go, the person behind the blindfolded person spins the blindfolded person three times and then points her in the correct direction. The person who spun the blindfolded person is the only one who can shout out

directions on how to progress across the course. If the blindfolded person touches a cone, she must count to 10 before she can resume walking. When the blindfolded person has crossed the field, the next participant taps her. The blindfolded player opens her eyes, gives the new player the blindfold, and goes to the end of the new line. Once the new player's blindfold is in place, the next person in line spins him three times and points him back across the field in the opposite direction. Once players have progressed to the opposite side of the room, they should sit down. The first team to complete the course wins that round.

In the second round, directions are shouted out by the teammate facing the blindfolded person on the opposite side of the line. This makes deciphering direction instructions much more difficult. In addition to multiple-voice distraction, there is also the problem of left and right distinction. When the instruction giver is facing in the same direction as the blindfolded player, left and right are true left and right. But, when the person giving instructions is facing the opposite direction, that player's left and right are opposite to that of the blind player. This problem may increase the time needed to complete the course.

Here are some questions you might use with your class or group after they've completed the activity:

- What were some of the special conditions that were presented?
- How might learning be affected as a result of the conditions represented in the game (that is, not being able to see, being disoriented by instructions coming from multiple directions, feeling pressure to move quickly under those conditions, and so forth)?
- What was the most frustrating part of this activity?
- Which part of the activity did you enjoy the most?
- How did you feel about giving directions?
- How did you feel about receiving directions and trusting others?
- Was round two more difficult than round one? If so, why?
- Did this activity make you feel any different about people who have special needs?

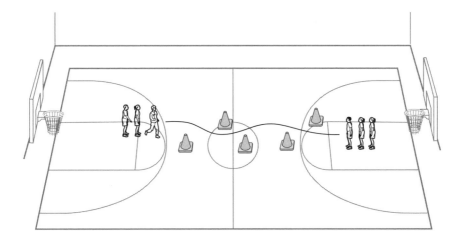

One Step Back, Two Steps Forward

AGES: Middle school through high school

EQUIPMENT: A piece of paper and writing implements

PURPOSE: The purpose of this activity is for young people to acknowledge their weaknesses—and, more important, their strengths—in various areas. Identifying twice the number of strengths as weaknesses and writing them down helps participants build confidence and self-esteem.

PROCEDURE: Participants are to think of a particular context (e.g., as an individual, in the physical realm, in the emotional realm, in the community, in the church, and so on) and write down a weakness they have in that area. After listing the weakness, they are asked to write down two strengths in the same area. This will help participants realize that, even if they're not exceptional in every area, they still have something positive to offer.

Here's an example:

Context: Sports (Basketball)

Weakness: I'm not a very fast runner.

Strength: I do have lots of endurance.

Strength: I am a good motivator for my team.

It might be a good idea to have participants answer the questions using several different contexts (as previously listed).

The Truth Does Matter

AGES: Middle school through high school

EQUIPMENT: Paper and writing implements

PURPOSE: This activity helps young people realize that honesty is an admirable character trait and that the trust others place in them is precious, yet can easily be lost.

PROCEDURE: Distribute paper and writing implements to the class or group. Read the following question aloud, and ask everyone in the group to write down their answers to each question. Afterward, ask volunteers to read their answers to each question.

- Have you ever been caught in a lie? If yes, how did you feel?
- Did the person you lied to react differently toward you afterward? Did you lose privileges as a result of the lie? Were you able to regain the person's trust?
- Have you ever been lied to by friends or loved ones? Did it affect your relationship with them?

Another way you can go with this activity is to ask participants to give examples of lies that have been exposed in professional sports. Then ask them to discuss the ways in which these lies have affected the sport and the athletes involved.

Peaceful Continuum

AGES: Middle school through high school

EQUIPMENT: List of problem-solving scenarios

PURPOSE: In this activity, young people think about how peacefully or aggressively they might react to various situations. The activity also gives participants an opportunity to share their beliefs with others in the class or group, and it allows for a thoughtful dialogue than can help everyone involved discover new ways to solve problems.

PROCEDURE: Once the teacher or group leader reads a scenario, participants go and stand in a place on an imaginary line that represents their reaction to the situation. "Peaceful" is at one end of the line, and "aggressive" is at the opposite end. If a person thought she would react to the situation in a totally peaceful manner, she'd stand at the beginning of the peace side of the line. If, however, she thought she might have a stronger reaction but wouldn't be all-out aggressive, she'd go and stand at about the halfway point on the line.

Once participants have chosen their spots in response to a scenario, the teacher or group leader asks for volunteers at both extreme sides of the line to explain why they feel the way they do. Then the teacher asks the group for suggestions as to how the aggressive person might become more peaceful.

Here are some scenarios you might use in this activity:

- Someone intentionally fouls you during a basketball game.
- The class bully tells you to move so he can take your seat during lunch.
- One of your classmates calls you stupid because you missed the ball.
- Someone is spreading rumors about you and another student in your PE class.
- You see someone stealing something out of your backpack.
- A couple of students are verbally harassing your best friend during break.

Blind-Faith Soccer

AGES: Middle school through high school

EQUIPMENT: 4 or 5 beach balls and 8 cones (for approximately 30 participants)

PURPOSE: The purpose of this activity is to help young people learn to work cooperatively with people who have special needs. It takes confidence in one's ability, as well as compassion, to effectively care for the safety of others.

PROCEDURE: The class or group should be divided into groups of three. A set of two cones should be placed at four different locations in the playing field. A gym is a good location for this activity.

Four groups of three players will be designated goalies. They will decide the width of their goal (placement of two cones) by raising their arms parallel to the ground and touching fingers. Goalies may be scored on in any direction, as long as the ball goes between the two cones and is shoulder height or lower. Goalies may use their hands to stop the ball from going through the goal. If a goal is stopped, the goalie may throw or bat the ball (with open hand) back into play. The goalie may not kick the ball.

Groups of three players, who are not goalies, connect themselves to each other by locking elbows. The middle player is blindfolded. The game starts with beach balls in a center location, away from the goals. Any of the three players may dribble the ball, but only the blindfolded player may score the goal. Players may also try to intercept balls that are in play, stopping other teams from scoring. No contact with other teams is permitted.

Once a goal is scored, the blindfolded player gives the blindfold to another teammate. A goal may not be scored against the same goalies two times in a row. The team must first score against another set of goalies. Give everyone a chance to be both a goalie and a blindfolded player. You may decide that, after a certain amount of time has passed, all nongoalies switch with the goalies. If a player doesn't feel comfortable being blindfolded, allow that player to pass on that position.

Here are some questions you might use to help your young people reflect on the activity once they've completed it:

- How did you feel about being blindfolded?
- Did you trust your teammates to keep you safe?
- How did they communicate with you?
- How did you feel about having the responsibility to watch out for the blind participant?
- Did you like this activity? Why or why not?

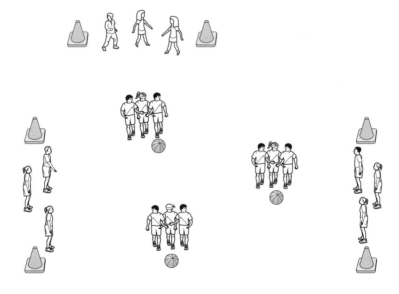

Your Actions Count!

AGES: Grade 4 through high school

EQUIPMENT: A sheet of paper to use as a scorecard

PURPOSE: This activity is intended to help participants become aware of how the comments that they and others make, both positive and negative, can affect the behavior of others.

PROCEDURE: In class, during any team activity where a score is kept, you might assign participants to be referees and scorekeepers. Without telling the players, the scorekeeper should keep track of all the positive and negative actions and words she observes during the game, recording them on a sheet of paper and noting whether they are positive or negative. For positive listings, 1 point is added to the score; for negative listings, 1 point is subtracted. At the end of the game, once the class assembles, the scorekeeper (without mentioning names) will read the positive and negative lists and give the final score. When the activity is complete, use the following questions for discussion:

- Do you prefer arguing or playing during a game?
- How do you settle arguments?
- How do negative comments affect physical performance?
- How do positive comments motivate a team?

Blind Shuffle

AGES: Grade 6 through high school

EQUIPMENT: None

PURPOSE: In this activity, young people work cooperatively—relying on their teammates—to complete a difficult task.

PROCEDURE: Divide your class or group into teams of five to six members. If there are six teams, the first person on each of the six teams remains seated, awaiting further instructions. Everyone else in the class or group stands up and spreads out in a designated area. The teacher or group leader asks the standing participants to close their eyes.

The players who have their eyes closed bend their elbows so that their palms are facing outward in front of their bodies to act as bumpers. Before starting the activity, the teacher or group leader has the seated players spread out along the edges or in the corners of the designated area. These players keep their eyes open and must stay in their designated spots. They are permitted to call out instructions to their teammates. Their objective is to help their teammates avoid collisions with the players on other teams.

On the signal to go, the players who are standing close their eyes. They start walking slowly around the room, calling out their team numbers, in search of the rest of their team. When teammates find each other, they must connect by hand or elbow and continue to find the rest of their team. Once all of the walking members of a team are connected, the teammates in the corners of the play area (the ones with eyes open) give directions on how to reach them. The first team to connect its "blind" members with its sighted member wins that round.

When the activity is complete, use the following questions for discussion:

- What made this activity difficult for both the "blind" and sighted members?
- Did you feel vulnerable?
- Would you prefer to be a leader or a follower? Why?
- What was the most effective way to communicate instructions?

Commitment to Your Team

AGES: Middle school through high school

EQUIPMENT: None

PURPOSE: In this activity, participants make a promise to their teammates and friends regarding their personal behavior and commitment. Before starting the activity, point out to your class or group that commitment to a team fosters confidence, strength, and camaraderie, all qualities that can enhance performance.

PROCEDURE: Have the participants answer these questions:

- Why should someone pick you to be on his or her team? (This is the time to brag about your good qualities.)
- What are you willing to offer your teammates to help ensure a positive environment for everyone?
- What are some of the expectations you have for others on the team?
- If you were the captain and the team were losing, how would you motivate the team?
- How might the answers to these questions be different if you substituted the word *friends* for *teammates?* What are the similarities?
- As a friend, are you willing to listen and to be respectful? Do you listen to your friends when they say no? Are you sensitive to their needs, not pressuring them to be the same as you are?

When the group has discussed the answers to the preceding questions, have participants fill out the following certificates: A Team Member's Promise, A Captain's Promise, and A Friend's Promise. These promises should be shared with others.

A Team Member's Promise

I, _____,

(your name here)

Promise to

_____

_____

_____

_____

_____

_____

_____

_____

_____

_____

_____

_____

_____

_____

_____

_____

_____

(continued)

From *Character-Building Activities: Teaching Responsibility, Interaction, and Group Dynamics* by Judy Demers, 2008, Champaign, IL: Human Kinetics.

(continued)

A Captain's Promise

I, _____,

(your name here)

Promise to

_____

_____

_____

_____

_____

_____

_____

_____

_____

_____

_____

_____

_____

_____

_____

_____

_____

_____

From *Character-Building Activities: Teaching Responsibility, Interaction, and Group Dynamics* by Judy Demers, 2008, Champaign, IL: Human Kinetics.

A Friend's Promise

I, _____,

(your name here)

Promise to

_____

_____

_____

_____

_____

_____

_____

_____

_____

_____

_____

_____

_____

_____

_____

_____

_____

_____

From *Character-Building Activities: Teaching Responsibility, Interaction, and Group Dynamics* by Judy Demers, 2008, Champaign, IL: Human Kinetics.

Say You're Sorry and Mean It!

AGES: Grade 4 through high school

EQUIPMENT: None

PURPOSE: This activity helps participants realize that when mistakes happen, they need to take responsibility for the consequences of their actions.

PROCEDURE: Before beginning the activity, lay some groundwork with your young people by presenting the following ideas: All of us make mistakes from time to time. Admitting our mistakes and learning to apologize for them can be difficult, yet admitting to ourselves that we aren't perfect—and learning from our mistakes—can make us stronger people. Like everything else, it takes practice to get good at it. Many hurt feelings could be eliminated with a simple apology for mistakes that are made.

Once you've presented some basic ideas about apologizing for mistakes and being sensitive to others' feelings, have participants act out the following scenarios (or make up their own). Each person plays the part of both the victim and the aggressor. Be sure the solution includes an effective apology.

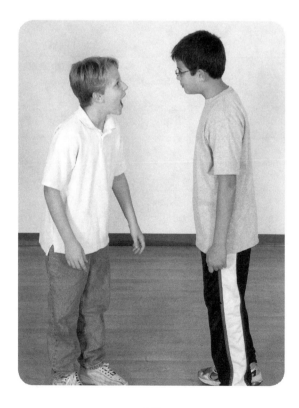

1. While returning the equipment after class, you threw the football across the gym. It hit someone in the back of the head.
2. You aggressively went for the basketball during a game and accidentally elbowed someone in the stomach.
3. When you tried to get through the door first, you tripped the person next to you.
4. You were given a red card for slide tackling in soccer.

After the group is finished acting out the various parts, you might give them this written assignment:

- Write about a time when it was hard for you to apologize. Did your lack of apology hurt your relationship with the other person or people?
- Was there a time when you wished that someone would apologize to you? Explain.
- Write about a time when someone apologized to you. How did you feel about the person before he or she apologized? How did you feel after the apology?

Attitude Is a Choice

AGES: Middle school through high school

EQUIPMENT: Attitude cards (one for each of the following attitudes listed) and cards with their definitions on them (one for each actor)

PURPOSE: The purpose of this activity is for young people to become aware of various attitudes and how they affect behavior. Participants should understand that, although they can't control everything that happens to them, they do have some control over how they react in certain situations.

PROCEDURE: Before starting this activity, go over the following attitudes and associated behaviors with your group. Cards should be made for each attitude and each definition.

Initiator: One who energetically begins or follows through with a task.

Instigator: A person who stirs things up and likes to see chaos.

Compromiser: Someone who sees multiple points of view and comes up with an agreement.

Reactor: A person who reacts to situations but doesn't contribute to solving problems.

Arbitrator: Someone who judges other people.

Deliberator: One who consults with others before coming to a decision.

Prosecutor: A person who seeks legal action against another person.

Sympathizer: One who feels or expresses compassion.

Procrastinator: Someone who always puts things off until tomorrow when they should be done today.

Pick nine volunteers, one for each attitude. Give each volunteer a definition of attitudes card (a card with the definitions of the preceding terms written on it). Ask volunteers to randomly pick an attitude by pulling an attitude card (one with only a specific attitude from the list written on it) and act out, with the group, one of the following scenarios. They should respond with their particular characteristic in mind. After the play is finished, ask the class or the whole group to identify the various attitude types.

1. Kenny in PE class has been bullying Sal. Sal doesn't want to be considered a snitch, but he doesn't know what to do. He has talked to his friends about the situation.

2. Jack intentionally sabotaged his team in the basketball game. His girlfriend was on the other team, and he wanted her team to win.

3. Someone threw a rock that hit a teacher's (coach's) car during basketball practice. The wrong person was blamed. Other athletes saw who threw it, but wouldn't come forward.

Here are some questions you might pose following the activity:

- Are some attitudes more acceptable than others? Why?
- If a person puts a lot of energy into something, does that always get the job done? Give examples that support your answer.

What Motivates You?

AGES: Middle school through high school

EQUIPMENT: None

PURPOSE: This activity helps young people understand different kinds of rewards and the effect that rewards have on motivation and persistence. Watching the skits they come up with can give you insight into the thoughts and needs of the young people you work with. You may see a little bit of yourself in the performances.

PROCEDURE: Preface this activity by presenting the following ideas to the group: Rewards and prizes motivate many of us; what happens to our will to persist when a reward is *not* involved? Motivation that comes from inside us, out of pure joy or passion, is called *intrinsic* motivation. Motivation that is driven by external rewards and outside sources is called *extrinsic* motivation. Intrinsic motivation helps lead to persistence and better equips us to overcome obstacles.
   Then, ask the group the following questions:

- What are some of the activities that you do for extrinsic reward?
- What are some of the activities that you do for intrinsic reward?

When the group has answered the questions, ask participants to think about positive and negative motivational strategies while acting out the following scenarios. The skits should portray both positive and negative motivation. Here are some scenarios:

1. Homework completion (negative and positive interaction with family members)
2. Sports practice (negative and positive coach interaction)
3. Schoolwork (negative and positive teacher interaction)

Reflection
Activities

Reflection is an important component of self-discovery, and self-discovery is one of the most meaningful ways to learn. Unlike instruction by lecture, self-discovery requires personal reflection, self-evaluation, and application. Self-discovery makes learning relevant and strengthens convictions. Young people are not always given opportunities to discuss and reflect on what they've learned, so personal meaning is sometimes lacking.

Although the activities in other chapters have a reflective component, the lessons here emphasize individual and group analysis and application. Activity lessons include social responsibility, individual rights, effective ways to communicate, general character development, teaching and critiquing, and goal setting.

Social Justice

AGES: All ages

EQUIPMENT: 1 Popsicle stick or chip for each participant

PURPOSE: In this activity, participants become more aware of how their actions affect the people around them. It is important for participants to know that this activity is in no way meant to be critical of any one person in the class or group; explain that it is meant to help make the group a safer and healthier environment for all its members. (I found that this activity made my students more aware of and accountable for their behavior. When I consistently allowed time for this activity, the social behavior of the class improved.)

PROCEDURE: Participants write their names on Popsicle sticks or chips, then the sticks or chips are put into a container. The teacher or group leader should stop the activity of the day with enough time to draw three names from the class container. When a participant's name has been drawn, the group is asked to contribute positive or negative interactions they have observed or

experienced regarding this person's behavior. Emphasize that the comments should be made in regard to the behavior and not the person. The leader informs the group that if no comments are made, or if comments are untrue, then no points can be earned toward the class total (all points are added to a class total for a reward day). 100 points are required to earn a free-option day. If remarks made are mostly positive, then the class earns 3 points. If comments are a mixture of positive and negative, then 2 points are earned. If comments are all negative, then 1 point is earned. The class votes on what the total should be for each person's behavior.

A physical education teacher designed this activity using Hellison's TPSR (teaching personal and social responsibility) model for teaching social skills (1995) as a guideline. I tried the activity with my sixth-grade class. I thought the class would not like the activity because it cut into the active play time for the day. To my surprise, the class enjoyed this time together. They would remind me if I didn't allow time for the sticks. Some of my students wrote in their journals that this was their favorite part of the day.

When I first introduced this activity, students were a little reluctant to speak about others' behavior that bothered them. After a short time, the students began to openly communicate their concerns. Some students were very surprised that so many people were affected by their behavior.

Character for the Day

AGES: Grade 3 through high school

EQUIPMENT: Cards or poker chips labeled with character traits

PURPOSE: This activity gives young people a fun, active way to identify and discuss one positive or negative character trait. It's a good, quick group warm-up and reflection activity.

PROCEDURE: This is a tag game that starts with several people who are "it." The taggers turn their backs to the group. The teacher or group leader gives one character trait card (or chip) to a participant. That person, and all of the other players, close one hand, to make it difficult to see who has the card. On the signal to go, all players scatter in a designated area (a basketball court is a good size). Nontaggers should give the card or chip (or pretend to) to other players. When a tagger touches someone, that person opens his hand. If he has the card or chip, he must give it to the teacher or group leader.

Once a tagger finds the card or chip, the round is over, and a discussion should begin. Here are some questions for discussion that you might use with your group:

- What does "dedicated" (or other trait) mean?
- What does "judgmental" (or other trait) look like?
- How does this trait affect people?
- How might aggressiveness (or other negative trait) be changed to a positive trait?

Example labels for character trait cards or chips:

Positive	Negative
compassionate	aggressive
trustworthy	dishonest
friendly	cold
dedicated	bored
disciplined	unruly
tolerant	intolerant
caring	boastful
courageous	cowardly
honest	judgmental
fair	argumentative
complimentary	jealous

Changing "You" to "I" Messages
(Effective Communication)

AGES: Grade 4 and up

EQUIPMENT: Copies of the handout and writing implements

PURPOSE: This activity is intended to help participants find appropriate and effective ways of communicating their displeasure with other people's behavior.

PROCEDURE: Ask the young people to change the following "you" messages to "I" messages, writing down their answers. (For example, change the statement "You are so lazy!" to "I am frustrated when you expect me to pick up after you. It makes me feel that you don't respect me.") Once everyone has finished, ask for volunteers to share their answers. You might ask participants to come up with their own scenarios and act them out in front of the whole group, then ask the group to discuss the effectiveness of each scenario.

1. You are so inconsiderate.
2. You're always taking my stuff.
3. You don't care about anything.
4. You always do what you want!

Having Privilege Doesn't Make It Better

AGES: Middle school through high school

EQUIPMENT: Paper and writing implements

PURPOSE: In this activity, young people will see that they don't need expensive, sophisticated equipment in order to learn, to have fun, and to be creative.

I once went to a motivational workshop that taught us how to get the most out of our available equipment. We were given one piece of paper and were told to use it to develop an activity that would last 40 to 45 minutes and would include at least half of the participants. I had more fun than I've had in a long time. I felt like I was a kid again. Thus was the idea for this activity born.

PROCEDURE: Instruct your class or group to think of an activity that could be done using only one piece of paper (see New Game Development in chapter 1). The activity needs to be active and to last approximately 40 minutes. Encourage participants to work in teams to design their activity or game (I would allow about 45 minutes for them to come up with ideas). If individuals or teams finish early, let them try their activity on others who are also finished. Once all activities are complete, give each team 10 to 15 minutes to present its activity to the whole group. Allow some people to be active participants while others are observers. Once the activity is presented, allow participants time to critique and give constructive criticism.

Discuss the following questions with your class or group:

- Was this a difficult activity? Why or why not?
- Were you challenged?
- Is it possible to have fun with minimal equipment?
- Describe a creative game you've played at home using little or no equipment.

Share stories of your own, as well. I tell my students about how, when I was very young, I could play all day with an empty dish-soap bottle I would fill with water. I would spray little circles of water, simulating stepping-stones that would allow me to walk safely in shark-infested waters or travel over quicksand in the jungle. The water had power to revive dead plants and awake sleeping insects, and I could drench my older brother from enough distance to make a speedy escape!

Don't Just Criticize—Be Constructive

AGES: Middle school through high school

EQUIPMENT: Copies of the handout

PURPOSE: This activity is intended to help young people realize that one kind of criticism is beneficial and another is hurtful. The lesson gives examples of both kinds of criticism.

Before starting the activity, consider holding a class or group discussion using these talking points:

- Criticism is much easier to give than to take, even when it's constructive.
- Constructive criticism addresses a person's actions; it is not a personal attack.
- Comments that are positive in nature can give people ideas about how to find ways to improve.
- Constructive criticism should be delivered using "I" statements. "I" statements (e.g., "I felt hurt when you were late for our date") are less threatening than are "you" statements (e.g., "You're so inconsiderate!").
- Don't criticize things that people can't change (physical ability and looks would fall into this category).

PROCEDURE: Distribute the handout. Ask participants to read the statements on the following list and to mark the Hurtful or Helpful column for each statement.

When they've finished marking their handouts, use these questions for discussion:

- How could you change one of the hurtful comments into helpful comments?
- What makes criticism hard to take?
- Has anyone ever gotten mad at you because of your criticism? Was there a better way to give the criticism?

Then pair off the participants, and have them practice giving and receiving constructive criticism using the following scenarios. Advise the receivers of the criticism to try to listen and not interrupt.

Adapted, by permission, from J.L. Skully, 2000, *The power of social skills in character development: Helping diverse learners succeed* (Port Chester, NY: Dude Publishing), 99.

- How to be a good team player
- How to improve conditioning
- How to stay relaxed before a competition
- How to improve your tennis serve
- How to increase your shooting accuracy in basketball

Don't Just Criticize—Be Constructive

Read the following statements. Mark the Hurtful or Helpful column for each statement.

	Hurtful	Helpful
If you follow through with your fingers pointing to the target, I believe you will be more accurate.	_____	_____
You should be more careful; you're getting sloppy.	_____	_____
It's not always about you—use your teammates.	_____	_____
You'll never be fast; you just don't have the body for it.	_____	_____
Relaxing your shoulders will help you be a more efficient runner.	_____	_____
I think if you try lifting light weights, you'll notice a difference.	_____	_____
Positive self-talk can keep you focused; I know it helped my game.	_____	_____
What were you thinking when you took that shot!	_____	_____

Adapted, by permission, from J.L. Skully, 2000, *The power of social skills in character development: Helping diverse learners succeed* (Port Chester, NY: Dude Publishing), 99.

From *Character-Building Activities: Teaching Responsibility, Interaction, and Group Dynamics* by Judy Demers, 2008, Champaign, IL: Human Kinetics.

Goal Setting

AGES: Middle school through high school

EQUIPMENT: None

PURPOSE: The purpose of this activity is to help young people plan for future success by setting effective, realistic goals.

PROCEDURE: This is a discussion activity. Use the following talking points, and solicit input from your class or group:

- It's hard to know where you're going if you don't have a plan to get there. Think about things in your life that you would like to accomplish or change.
- Don't be afraid to set challenging goals for yourself, but at the same time, be realistic. For example, it wouldn't be feasible to tell yourself that you'll run a marathon next week if you have never trained for one.
- Setting short-term and long-term goals can help you monitor your progress and plan for success.
- Goal setting is a way of making a commitment to yourself. Goals help to motivate, lead to feelings of success if achieved, help build self-esteem, provide a way for you to measure your progress, help you focus your effort and intention, and lead to long-term persistence.
- Effective goals should be SMART (Weinberg & Gould, 1999). The acronym stands for *specific, measurable, action-oriented, realistic,* and *timely.*
- Goals should be revisited. You'll need to modify them if you're not making progress or are not meeting your milestones. There's no point in beating yourself up if you tried your best and were not successful. Just assess the situation, decide what you can realistically achieve, and go from there.
- Don't measure your success by the accomplishments or approval of others. You can't control anyone else's thoughts or actions. Comparing yourself with others can be frustrating at best.
- What is a short-term goal (something in the next few weeks to several months) that you would like to accomplish?
- What is a long-term goal (something in the next year or several years) that you would like to accomplish?

Fair Teams?

AGES: Grade 4 through high school

EQUIPMENT: None

PURPOSE: The purpose of this activity is to give participants an opportunity to find creative, equitable ways to pick team members. Choosing teams that make everyone happy is almost impossible. I try to find ways that will balance abilities, so that games will be more challenging. It's important to be inclusive and nonthreatening when picking teams. Try to separate any cliques that occur with team members. Look for teachable moments when you see participants being unfair with others.

PROCEDURE: Ask your class or group for ideas about how to pick fair teams. If the ideas do not seem fair, ask leading questions that address the issue. For example, if a suggestion were to have captains pick the teams, you might ask the following questions:

- How do you think the last people picked would feel?
- If all of the skilled players are on the same team, how will the less-skilled players get any better?

If students or group members come up with good ideas, using them can be a validating experience. You might even want to try ideas that you don't think will work. However, don't stay with the same teams too long when the combination of team members is not a positive experience. An open discussion with your students, excluding names, about what worked and what didn't can be beneficial to everyone in the group.

Once teams are formed, it's a good idea for members to sign a team commitment contract. (See Commitment to Your Team in chapter 2.)

Team Together

AGES: Grade 2 and up

EQUIPMENT: None

PURPOSE: In this activity, each child has a chance to make a positive contribution that benefits the entire group, and each has a chance to be both a leader and a follower.

PROCEDURE: This activity is a good way for teams to warm up and be energized. Each team or squad should stand in a line with one person behind the other. Each person on the team needs to come up with a movement or stretch that can be completed from his or her position in the line. (Movements should not be embarrassing or too difficult for anyone in the class to perform.)

On the signal to begin, the first person in a team's line performs one movement or stretch, and then everyone else in that team's line does likewise. The first person then runs to the back of the line. Person 2 completes the first person's movement and then adds a movement of her own. The entire team

then performs these movements. Person 2 then runs to the end of the line. Everyone in the line should complete the prior movement or movements before adding one of their own. If time allows, let each team share the exercises for the entire class or group to perform.

Each time you do this activity, you might want to change the order of the team members in the lines so that the same people aren't always going first or last.

In order to help with this activity, you might want to discuss the purpose of stretching. Emphasize that the body should be warm before stretching. Showing examples of specific stretches for the activity you are doing would be beneficial. You might want to discuss contraindicated stretches—ones that could potentially cause injury to the body. You might also want to mention the stretching techniques listed here:

- Static: stretching to the furthest point and then holding
- Ballistic: involves bobbing and rebounding movements (can lead to injury)
- Dynamic: moving through range of motion without bouncing or jerky movement
- After doing the activity, you might ask your group questions like:
- How did you feel about this type of warm-up?
- Did making up your own movements make you feel important?
- Did the members of the team feel more connected? Why or why not?

Ask for Help

AGES: All ages

EQUIPMENT: None

PURPOSE: The purpose of this discussion activity is for young people to understand that everyone needs help from time to time. Realizing that we're not all on our own can relieve us of unnecessary stress.

PROCEDURE: Explain to the class or group that it's not a weakness to ask for help; it just means that we are human. In many cases, the person who is asked to help feels honored that they can be of service. False assumptions can be made when people won't ask for help. As a teacher, I sometimes assume that when students don't ask, they understand what I'm teaching—and that's not always the case. Some students may be embarrassed, or they may think that their question is stupid.

As a follow-up to the discussion, give your group the following assignment:

> Get used to asking questions. When you go home today, ask one of your parents or a sibling a question that you would like answered.

What Is a Hero? (Handling Adversity)

AGES: Grade 3 and up

EQUIPMENT: None

PURPOSE: This activity helps participants think about people in their lives who have overcome obstacles and have not given up in the face of adversity. *A Hero in Every Heart,* by H. Jackson Brown, Jr. and Robyn Spizman, is a great inspirational book that talks about how athletes succeed when most others would give up.

PROCEDURE: Ask your group what a hero is. Be prepared for answers such as Superman, Spiderman, and so forth. When they've finished answering, share a story about a hero of yours. Here is one that I tell:

April was a 3-year-old girl who was born with a rare blood disease. When she was born, her fingers were webbed together. Every 6 months or so, she needed surgery on her hands to separate her fingers. April wore thick corduroy pants, mittens on her hands, and slippers on her feet. Anything rough against her skin would cause bleeding. April was never careful. She was always running and playing and had a smile on her face. She would sometimes fall and you could see the blood seep through her clothes. Sometimes April would be lying on the floor in fetal position due to extreme abdominal pain.

When I finish the story, I ask my students why they think someone with so many health problems would be so active and so happy. This usually leads to some good conversation. Here's another hero story that I tell:

When I was in my early twenties, I was trying to make the Olympic team in track and field. One of my mentors was a coach who was a quadriplegic (a person who can't move his arms or legs). Before he contracted polio at age 24, he was one of the best speed skaters in the country. Although he needed a wheelchair for mobility, he was one of the strongest people I ever met. I know he was in terrible pain, but he never complained. He would write me the most inspirational letters whenever I got down on myself. Although he had no experience with high jumping, he would wheel himself through the library, studying numerous books and techniques. He would interview the best coaches and go observe them when he could. He ended up coaching his daughter to become the youngest female Olympic high jumper in history. What an amazing man!

When you've finished with your stories, ask the participants if they know of a hero that they would like to tell the group about. Some of my students have shared personal stories for the very first time during this activity. A student in one of my classes told about a classmate who was his hero, and the other students gained a new respect for that unassuming member of the class as a result.

Finally, ask the participants who they would be if they could be any hero they wanted to be, and why.

Character or Not

AGES: Middle school through high school

EQUIPMENT: Character label cards and character definition cards

PURPOSE: The purpose of this activity is to give young people an opportunity to experience various character traits and to discuss the effect these qualities have on others.

PROCEDURE: As an introduction to the activity, ask participants if they know the meaning of the word *character*. If they do not know the definition, tell them that it's what makes a person who he is. Then ask them what the qualities of "good" character are. You can refer to the following list in this discussion.

According to Koehler and Royer (2001), there are six qualities of good character:

1. Unconditionally friendly most of the time
2. Free from inner anger
3. Committed to working for causes and events (vigorously and confidently)
4. Self-controlled
5. Compliant with rules and regulations
6. Aware of consequences of behavior

Ask each participant to find a partner. Randomly hand out one card, along with a list of definitions, to each set of partners. Character cards should be labeled as follows: honesty, wealth, charity, power, family, freedom, courage, friendship, faith, morality, possessions, fame, status, wisdom, honor, competition, hard work, consideration, and compassion. Instruct one person in each pair to pretend that he or she is a famous athlete (it doesn't matter in which sport) and to have a conversation emphasizing the word on the card. The partner must try to guess what the character trait on the card is.

After each partner has had a chance to play the part of the athlete, the teacher or leader should choose volunteers to speak in front of the whole group. Each volunteer is given a different word to represent. Volunteers, one at a time, have a conversation with the group, pretending to be famous athletes. The leader then asks the class if they thought the presenter possessed a positive or a negative character trait.

If the class thinks the conversation deals with a negative trait, ask if they can think of a way to make it positive. An example might be that someone who is famous and conceited could use his fame to help promote a worthy cause.

Here's a list of definitions for the character traits:

Honesty: being truthful
Wealth: abundance of possessions
Charity: something given to help the needy
Power: strength or force
Family: a group sharing common ancestry
Freedom: without restraints
Courage: being brave even in frightening or intimidating circumstances
Friendship: caring about someone else
Faith: belief in something
Morality: right or good conduct
Possessions: things that you own
Fame: wide recognition
Status: your place in society
Wisdom: experience combined with intelligence
Honor: special esteem or respect
Competition: rivalry for a profit or prize
Hard work: challenging
Consideration: kindness
Compassion: deep feeling of sharing the suffering of others

Role Models

AGES: Grade 4 and up

EQUIPMENT: None

PURPOSE: In this activity, participants are asked to think about their expectations of a variety of people and about the responsibilities to others they think those people have.

PROCEDURE: Ask your class or group to think about what they look for in each of the following role models, and discuss the answers:

Parent
Older sibling
Physical education teacher
Police officer
Famous athlete
Rock star

Then ask the following questions:

- What makes a good role model?
- Are you a good role model? Why or why not?
- Can you think of a celebrity who is a positive role model? Why is this person a good role model? Can you think of a celebrity who is a negative role model? Why is this person not a good role model? How could this person change negative behavior into positive behavior?

Labels

AGES: Grade 4 and up

EQUIPMENT: Paper and writing implements

PURPOSE: This activity is designed to make participants aware of the words people use to label other people. It demonstrates for children that labels can be hurtful and harmful and are often a way of stereotyping people and trying to control them.

PROCEDURE: Ask the class or group what labels others have given them (or they've given themselves). Discuss whether the labels are positive or negative. Then have them list the words they've been labeled with on one half of a sheet of paper and related positive statements across from the words. For example, one label might be "I'm boring." A positive statement in response to that could be, "I am very creative. I come up with original and interesting ideas that others like."

What's in a Promise?

AGES: Grade 4 and up

EQUIPMENT: Paper and writing implements

PURPOSE: The purpose of this activity is to make young people aware of the importance of the promises they make—both to themselves and to other people—and of keeping those promises in order to maintain their integrity.

PROCEDURE: Pass out a handout that lists the following questions and ask participants to write their answers on the paper.

1. Describe a promise that you made and kept. Was it easy or hard to keep the promise? Explain in detail.
2. Describe a promise that you didn't keep. What made it difficult to follow through? What did you say to the person or people involved? What was their reaction to your broken promise? Would you do anything different next time?
3. Write down a promise that you want to make to yourself—something that will help you in the area of health, fitness, or nutrition. Example: "I promise I'll stretch 3 days a week."
4. Write down a helpful promise you could make to someone else. Example: "I will help you with your homework," or "I will teach you how to skate."

Ask your students to share their answers. Sharing with others can help strengthen individual's commitment to keep their promises.

Forgive Yourself and Your Neighbor

AGES: Middle school through high school

EQUIPMENT: Paper and writing implements

PURPOSE: This activity helps young people learn the benefits of offering forgiveness to others and allows them to explore ways of doing so by acting out various real-life scenarios.

PROCEDURE: Lead a discussion about forgiveness with your class or group, using these talking points:

According to the *Complete Idiot's Guide to Enhancing Self-Esteem* (Warner, 1999), these are some of the benefits of forgiving others:

- Releases negative emotional energy
- Helps healing
- Allows you to give to another person
- Helps you serve as a role model
- Helps create a better society
- Gives peace of mind

Point out that it is as important to forgive ourselves for our mistakes as it is to forgive others when they have wronged us, but that it's often more difficult to do so.

Following the lead-in discussion, have the young people get into groups and write a skit about a sport setting where people aren't willing to forgive each other (or themselves). Then have them rewrite such that the skits show forgiveness in action. Ask for volunteers to act out the skits.

After the skits, have participants think about something that they have not been willing to forgive themselves for. Then, on a piece of paper, have them answer the following questions:

- Why aren't you willing to forgive yourself?
- What benefit is there in not forgiving yourself?

Answering these difficult questions might be an emotional experience for some. You may ask if anyone would like to share answers. Respect their privacy, if individuals are unwilling to share out loud. Ask the students who shared if it felt good to share.

Share Your Talents

AGES: Grade 4 and up

EQUIPMENT: None

PURPOSE: This activity shows young people that they have a lot to offer and that they can make a positive difference in others' lives.

PROCEDURE: Lead a discussion with your class or group on the topic of gifts we can give to others. You might use the talking points that follow:

Winston Churchill once said, "You make a living by what you get, you make a life by what you give." If you are able to walk, talk, listen, or show compassion, you have gifts to share. I remember watching an athlete at the Special Olympics. This young man was in a wheelchair. He was in a track meet throwing the javelin. He had no legs and just stubs for arms. He balanced the javelin on top of his shoulder and under his chin. He was able to torque his body and fling the javelin forward. This young man was an amazing athlete who shared his gift of strength with me.

Helping others can add to your own feelings of self-worth. Sharing your talents can give others strength and perseverance. You can make a difference in someone else's life!

When you've finished the discussion, have your group do and then write about the following experiences, so they can be shared with the rest of the group upon completion:

1. At home, teach a family member something helpful you learned at school.
2. What is something you learned at school that you could teach?
3. Reach outside the family. What's a good deed you could do for someone in the neighborhood or in the community?
4. Think of others who have volunteered in your life. What pleasures did they bring you?
5. What's your fondest memory of an act of kindness directed toward you?

Fight for a Cause

AGES: Middle school through high school

EQUIPMENT: None

PURPOSE: To show young people that one person can make a difference and that many important changes that have happened in the world resulted from the initial efforts of one person. An example of how one person made a difference is how Martin Luther King, Jr., one of the main leaders of the American civil rights movement, was able to fight for peace and equality in a non-aggressive manner. Historical changes occurred as a result of one man's dream.

PROCEDURE: Ask students or group members what they are passionate about:

- Do you enjoy exercise, clean beaches, and clean air? You could organize a beach or trail cleanup project. Or you might convince your friends to ride their bikes rather than driving or riding in motor vehicles during a "spare the air" day.
- What's a cause you could fight for?
- How could you organize others to help you?
- What difference could you make?

Be Decisive!

AGES: Middle school through high school

EQUIPMENT: None

PURPOSE: In this activity, young people are encouraged to consider the idea that they can choose for themselves in many areas, and that they have the right do to so even if their decision is not the popular one.

PROCEDURE: Lead a discussion about decision making with your class or group. You might use the following talking points to guide the discussion:

Many of life's decisions are made for us, such as when to get to school and the appropriate ages to drive and vote. However, we often give up certain of the rights we do have, even at a young age. For example, we may let others decide our fashion choices or our entertainment preferences. Going along with choices that others label as "cool" inhibits our individual uniqueness.

Some of the choices we have are behavioral. We cannot always predict what will happen to us, but we can often choose the reaction we will have to certain events. Believe it or not, choosing *not* to react is a choice: If you see someone in need but you don't do anything because you don't want to get involved, you made a choice.

With the freedom of choice comes empowerment. If we take an active role in the choices we make regarding our health, for instance, we can assume responsibility for our future well-being.

After discussion, ask your group to think about the following questions:

- Do you always go along with the crowd? Are you confident enough to tell a friend, "No, I don't want to do that—it's not right for me"?
- What are some choices you make regarding your health, nutrition, or fitness?
- What are some choices you have regarding your education?

What's Your Passion?

AGES: Middle school through high school

EQUIPMENT: None

PURPOSE: Unless we exercise our freedom of choice, it's sometimes difficult to find out what we're passionate about. Passion doesn't usually come from necessity. When people truly love doing something, its not because of the rewards they'll receive or because they'll get approval from others. In this activity, young people share their passions and discover both their similarities to each other and their uniqueness as individuals.

PROCEDURE: Ask participants to communicate with others in the class or group to find out their passion. Advise the participants to:

- ask questions that will elicit detailed answers;
- be sure to listen closely to the person they're interviewing;
- make eye contact with the person they're interviewing; and
- ask clarifying questions, if they don't understand something the interviewee has said.

Give the group 15 minutes to interview and be interviewed by as many classmates or other group members as possible.

   When the group is finished with the interviews, you might use the following questions for discussion:

- What did you learn about passion?
- What did people in the class have in common?
- What was unique about people in the class?

Respect: Learned or Earned?

AGES: Grade 4 and up

EQUIPMENT: Paper and writing implements

PURPOSE: In this activity, young people think about what respect means to them. Discussion questions will explore the issues of how respect is gained and lost.

PROCEDURE: Ask the class or group to define respect and give examples. I know for myself, when I was on a track team, I had a very strict coach. He wanted total control and did not show respect for any of his athletes. I did what he asked out of fear, but I did not respect him. Respect is much like physical conditioning; once you lose it, it is very difficult to regain. With that in mind, think before you speak or act.

Hand out a paper with the following questions to be answered in writing:

- Is fear a way to gain respect?
- How can you gain respect?
- Is there a time when you lost respect for someone else? Have you regained respect for this person? Why or why not?
- Showing respect may be as simple as acknowledging someone with a smile. Who did you make smile today? What did you do?
- Has anyone ever lost respect for you?
- What makes it difficult to regain respect?

When they're done, ask the group if they would like to share answers with others.

Dream Team

AGES: Middle school through high school

EQUIPMENT: None

PURPOSE: The purpose of this activity is to help students think about admirable qualities in a person.

PROCEDURE: Ask students or group members what kind of person they think they would be able to depend on if their lives were at stake. What qualities would they want such a person to have? In addition, have them think about their own admirable qualities; the qualities they bring to others. Then ask them to imagine that they're playing a game in which the result is a life-or-death situation. If their team does not succeed, everyone on the team dies. Allow each person to pick five people (the people can be living or can be historical figures) to be on the team.

Ask for volunteers to share the details of the game and whom they chose. This could lead to an interesting class discussion.

Being Responsible

AGES: Middle school through high school

EQUIPMENT: Paper and writing implements

PURPOSE: In this activity, participants think about the responsibilities of various people in their lives.

PROCEDURE: Distribute paper and ask participants to list the responsibilities they think each of the following people have:

A coach	An entertainer
A parent	A model
A student	A counselor
A friend	A babysitter
A teacher	An older brother or sister
An adult	A police officer
A professional athlete	You

When the responsibility list is complete, ask individuals to share their answers with the group. Ask if they think certain groups have similar responsibilities.

How Do You Handle Stress?

AGES: Middle school through high school

EQUIPMENT: None

PURPOSE: The purpose of this activity is threefold: to make young people aware that everyone experiences stress in their lives, that people handle stress in a variety of ways, and that there are more- and less-healthy stress-reducing techniques.

PROCEDURE: Ask students or group members to interview at least three people and find out what kinds of stress they experience and how they handle it. (At least one of the people interviewed must be an adult.) You can give the participants suggestions for various people they might interview. For example, they could interview:

A coach

A teacher

A parent

A friend

A student

A musician

A brother or sister

When the students have done their interviews, ask if they noticed any similarities in the type of stress shared by different groups. Was there a similar way of handling stress among groups?

Profess Your Profession

AGES: Middle school through high school

EQUIPMENT: Paper and writing implements

PURPOSE: The purpose of this assignment is to help young people realize that all professions have certain requirements and preparation.

PROCEDURE: Distribute copies of a handout containing the following questions or have your class or group write them down:

- What is your ideal profession? Why?
- What training is required? (Some research may be required to answer this question properly.)
- How will you meet the requirements?

Once participants have completed their research and have answered the questions, have a sharing session in which they tell others in the group what the requirements are for their chosen profession (without naming the profession) and how they think they could meet the requirements, and let others guess which profession they are talking about.

Freedoms

AGES: Middle school through high school

EQUIPMENT: None

PURPOSE: This activity is designed to make young people aware of the fact that not everyone has the same freedoms.

PROCEDURE: Discuss the following questions with your class or group:

- What freedoms do we have? Are they based on age or sex? If so, explain.
- What responsibilities come with freedom?
- How do we let others take away our freedoms?
- How can we effectively fight for our freedoms or the freedoms of others? (Ask participants to consider the marginalized and people without a voice).

Gender Matters

AGES: Middle school through high school

EQUIPMENT: None

PURPOSE: In this activity, young people have an opportunity to explore the various ways in which people are treated, depending on their gender.

PROCEDURE: Discuss the following questions with your class or group:

- What is gender bias?
- What are examples of gender bias?
- Should people treat you differently because of gender? Why or why not?
- Are expectations different for each gender? Why or why not? Is it changing?
- Is there gender equity in sports? If not, should there be? Why or why not?
- Does the society a person lives in determine what is acceptable?
- Does a person's cultural background affect what is acceptable?
- What expectations do you have of yourself? What expectations does your family have of you?
- What is a stereotype? (Ask participants to give some examples.)
- Why do stereotypes persist?
- What are some examples of gender stereotypes in sports?

Have Faith

AGES: Middle school through high school

EQUIPMENT: None

PURPOSE: This activity allows young people to define what faith means to them.

PROCEDURE: You may want to introduce this activity by using the following talking points:

- Faith refers to something that you believe in, as opposed to something you can see and explain.
- Many people live their lives guided by a strong faith.
- Some people feel that their faith makes them strong and helps them endure difficult situations.

Then discuss the following questions with your class or group:

- What does faith mean to you?
- What makes people believe in things they have not physically seen?
- Where does faith come from?

Share Your Gift

AGES: Grade 3 through high school

EQUIPMENT: Enough clothespins labeled with a positive character trait so that every participant can have one. Duplicate traits are permitted.

PURPOSE: This activity is designed to help participants think about the gifts that they possess, share them with the less fortunate, and realize that sharing can add value to their lives.

PROCEDURE: To begin the activity, make sure you have a clothespin with a positive character trait written on it for each participant (you might ask the group to come up with ideas for labeling the clothespins). Ask participants to sit down, close their eyes, and open their hands behind their backs. Tell participants that many of them will receive multiple clothespins and some will receive none. If a clothespin is placed in a participant's hands, she can open her eyes to pin it (or them, if she gets more than one) to one or both sleeves.

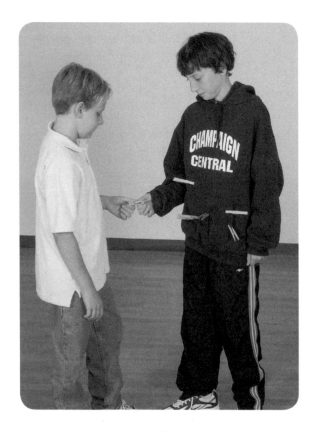

The teacher or group leader distributes multiple clothespins to approximately one-third of the participants, then instructs the participants to open their eyes, stand up, and start walking around in a designated area. The area should only be large enough for the group to comfortably walk around in without bumping into others (half a basketball court is a good size for a group of 30). Participants who have multiple clothespins should give a clothespin to someone who doesn't have one. The activity is over when everyone is wearing a clothespin.

After the activity, you might lead a discussion using these questions:

- How did you feel when you were given multiple clothespins?
- Were you selective about giving away your clothespins? If so, why?
- How did you feel when you weren't given any clothespins?
- What did it feel like when you were helping others?
- How did it feel when someone else helped you?
- Did you feel any different after you received a clothespin?

False Assumptions

AGES: Middle school through high school

EQUIPMENT: None

PURPOSE: This activity is designed to help young people express feelings of being misjudged by others. In expressing those feelings, they may become more receptive to the needs of others.

PROCEDURE: Lead the class or group in a discussion about being misjudged. You might share a story from your own experience to start things off. When I do this activity with my classes, these are the examples I share:

I once had a teacher who told me I was selfish for not sharing my ideas with the rest of the class. Some of my former classmates thought I was "stuck up," because I wasn't very social. They didn't realize that I was very shy. I was also told that I would never be a very good athlete, because I didn't have the so-called killer instinct. Well, I got to compete all over the world without that instinct. Thirty years ago, my supervising teacher told me I would never be good at teaching because I thought too much of my students. All of those people made false assumptions about me.

After sharing your personal experience, ask the people in your class or group to talk about theirs. You might use the following questions:

- Do you have any examples of situations in which someone misjudged you? (You can relate it to sports, if you wish.)

- Do you have any examples of situations in which you misjudged someone else?

Don't Take It Personally

AGES: Middle school through high school

EQUIPMENT: Paper and writing implements

PURPOSE: This activity helps young people realize that we don't always know why people react the way they do.

PROCEDURE: Relate the following scenario to your class or group: Imagine that your best friend, who's the captain of your basketball team, drastically changes his or her behavior. This person no longer seems to care for the team and easily becomes angry with everyone. The team wants you to be the new captain.

Once you've described the scenario, pose these questions to the group, and have them write their answers on a piece of paper:

- What would you do in this situation?
- What steps would you take to resolve the problem?
- How could you help the situation and still remain friends with the captain?

Then ask for volunteers who want to discuss their answers. During the ensuing discussion, you might also point out that it's easy to be offended when best friends snap at you or want to be left alone, but that their behavior may have nothing to do with you—it may be the result of a personal struggle they're having. Suggest that this might be a time when the friend needs you most.

Accusations Hurt!

AGES: Middle school through high school

EQUIPMENT: Paper and writing implements

PURPOSE: In this activity, young people learn that accusations are serious and are an affront to a person's character.

PROCEDURE: In order to illustrate the hurt that wrongful accusations can cause, you might want to share a story from your own experience. This is one that I use:

At one time, I taught physical education at an elementary school. We were outside before lunch, so all the lunch bags were lined up along the sideline of the basketball court. At lunchtime, Johnny realized that something was missing from his lunch. He came up crying and said, "Tommy stole something from my lunch!" Well, he wouldn't tell me what was missing, and he hadn't actually seen Tommy take anything. Of course, Tommy denied it. I began lecturing the class about honesty. I also said it's not right to blame someone for something that wasn't witnessed. In the middle of my discussion, pieces of chocolate cake began to fall from the sky. The seagulls were the guilty ones, and they didn't stick around for the lecture. Johnny was embarrassed, and Tommy was upset.

After relating your experience of a person or people being wrongly accused, you might use these questions for discussion:

- If you feel you're wronged by someone, what is a more appropriate way to handle the problem than to immediately accuse them of the wrongdoing?

- If you thought that a friend of yours had done something wrong, what would you do?

- Ask if any individuals would like to share their answers. Perhaps members of the group could show their answers by acting out a skit.

Respect Is a Two-Way Street

AGES: Middle school through high school

EQUIPMENT: The handout and writing implements

PURPOSE: The purpose of this activity is to help young people understand that respect needs to be earned and is easily lost.

PROCEDURE: Lead a discussion with your class or group on the topic of respect. You might use the following talking points to guide the discussion.

- Respect should not be demanded. Instilling fear in people may command their obedience, but it doesn't create respect.
- Respect is an honor earned by treating someone fairly and admirably. Think about how you want to be treated. Is it fair to be disrespectful to others, then turn around and demand respect from them?
- Respect doesn't mean you have the same rights, privileges, or responsibilities as everyone else. Your older brother or sister may be able to stay out later than you can, but that doesn't mean your parents don't respect you. Expectations may be different for different maturity levels.

After the discussion, distribute the "respect chart" to your group and give participants some time to fill it out. Then ask for volunteers to share their written answers.

Respect Is a Two-Way Street

From	Toward	Ways of show-ing respect	Ways of losing respect
You	Parent		
You	Sibling		
You	Teacher		
You	Coach		
Parent	You		
Sibling	You		
Teacher	You		
Coach	You		

From *Character-Building Activities: Teaching Responsibility, Interaction, and Group Dynamics* by Judy Demers, 2008, Champaign, IL: Human Kinetics.

Give Someone a Jump Start

AGES: Middle school through high school

EQUIPMENT: Paper and writing implements

PURPOSE: In this activity, young people are encouraged to look beyond their personal needs by becoming aware of people who are weakened in some way, oppressed, or even silenced.

PROCEDURE: Give students or group members the following assignment:

- Without giving names, write about a situation in which you helped make life better for someone else. Describe the situation in detail. Do you think your help made a difference? How did you feel about the experience?

- Have you seen situations in your physical education class where students are being overpowered or weakened? Did you see anyone try to help the people involved?

Excuses Don't Get the Job Done

AGES: Middle school through high school

EQUIPMENT: Paper and writing implements

PURPOSE: In this activity, young people think about how they deal with obstacles and learn ways of overcoming them.

PROCEDURE: Lead a class or group discussion about how people handle challenges and obstacles to success. You might use the following points as a lead-in to the discussion:

Many of us feel the need to make excuses for not living up to high expectations. We often place these expectations on ourselves and then feel pressured to live up to them. Excuses give us an easy way out for not trying our best, or not trying at all. We need to learn to set reasonable goals—goals that allow us to monitor our progress and appreciate our successes. Exercising the power of positive thinking helps us find ways of being successful rather than excuses for failure.

After introducing the topic of obstacles and excuses, ask participants to write answers to the following questions contained in a handout:

- What are some excuses you've made regarding the physical aspects of your life (sports, exercise, nutrition, or other)?
- What are some excuses you've made regarding your behavior?

List ways of changing these excuses into positive actions:

Excuse: I can't help getting mad when my team loses; I'm just a competitive person.

Positive action:

Excuse: There's no way I would try out for the track team; I'm too slow.

Positive action:

Excuse: I could be the best one in the class, if I wanted to be.

Positive action:

Adapted, by permission, from J.L. Skully, 2000, *The power of social skills in character development: Helping diverse learners succeed* (Port Chester, NY: Dude Publishing), 177.

Rules Were Made to Be Followed

AGES: Grade 4 through high school

EQUIPMENT: None

PURPOSE: The purpose of this activity is to help participants understand the importance of making and following rules and the fact that most rules are made in order to promote safety and fairness.

PROCEDURE: When you go over the rules for an activity, check for understanding and ask participants if they would like to add or change any rules. Also, discuss the consequences for breaking the rules. Once there's unanimous agreement, ask the class or group to sign a contract stating that they'll abide by the rules of fair play. If rules are being broken, use the contract as a teaching moment to discuss commitment and consequences.

You might use these questions for discussion:

- What are some of your family rules? Are there different rules for different members of the family?
- Are there rules that you think *you* don't need to follow, but others should? Why is this?
- Are there rules that you should not follow (rules of initiation or sworn secrecy that could harm you or someone else, for example)?
- What do the rules for sports and the rules we follow in society have in common?

Psychological Benefit of Sports

AGES: Middle school through high school

EQUIPMENT: Paper and writing implements

PURPOSE: In this activity young people learn about their four basic psychological needs, and they identify how sports can help meet those needs.

PROCEDURE: Discuss the four basic psychological needs with your class or group. Those needs are as follows:

1. Relationship—belonging to a group and having connections to others that are based on love, cooperation, and caring
2. Capability—having the power to set goals and work on improvement
3. Independence—having the power to make our own decisions
4. Pleasure—entertaining ourselves and finding joy

Then have participants write down a list of ways that sports can help fulfill each of their psychological needs. When finished, ask participants to share their answers with the rest of the group.

Adapted, by permission, from J.L. Skully, 2000, *The power of social skills in character development: Helping diverse learners succeed* (Port Chester, NY: Dude Publishing), 143.

Conflict Resolution

AGES: Middle school through high school

EQUIPMENT: None

PURPOSE: In this activity, young people identify problems and find acceptable ways to resolve them.

PROCEDURE: Talk to your class or group about conflict and the various approaches to it. You can use the following talking points to ensure that participants understand the approaches:

There are three main ways to deal with conflict: passively, aggressively, or assertively. If you are passive, you tend to not speak your mind and let people take advantage of you. If you are aggressive, you demand that people treat you with respect. If you are assertive, you stand up for yourself but still show respect toward others. Some people switch behavior styles, or use a combination of styles, depending on the situation.

Then, read the following scenario to the group, and have them decide which style of conflict resolution is being used in each of three possible situations:

John is bumped while he and another player are going for the basketball. In response,

John elbows the other player to gain control of the ball. (aggressive)

John ignores the contact and continues to play. (passive)

John tells the player, "Hey, watch the contact!" and then continues to play. (assertive)

After participants have decided which style of conflict resolution John used in each case, you could ask them why they think a person would react in those various ways. Ideas that might be mentioned include the following: If John had low self-esteem, and believed that whatever happened to him didn't matter, he might take a passive stance and do nothing. If John believed in winning at all costs, he might react aggressively and get too physical. Or, if he felt good about himself and was aware of this conflict-resolution option, John might stand up for his rights in an assertive way. Ask your group what the probable outcomes (consequences) might be in each case.

Finally, wrap up by asking participants to come up with conflict scenarios of their own (sports-related) and act out ways to solve the problem. Have the group determine whether the solution illustrates passive, aggressive, or assertive behavior.

Adapted, by permission, from J.L. Skully, 2000, *The power of social skills in character development: Helping diverse learners succeed* (Port Chester,NY: Dude Publishing), 151.

Initiate, Don't Just React

AGES: Middle school through high school

EQUIPMENT: The "Do You Initiate or Respond?" handout, writing implements, and paper

PURPOSE: The purpose of this activity is to help young people understand that their contributions can make this world a better place.

PROCEDURE: Encourage participants to take the first step and initiate an action by doing a good deed. Examples of good deeds that you might mention include helping someone in need, acknowledging someone's presence, or praising someone for her accomplishments. Ask them to write about their experiences, answering the following questions in their report:

- Was doing this good deed difficult for you?
- How did the person react to you?
- How did you feel after you did it?

Do You Initiate or Respond?

Initiate	Respond
You are usually the first to smile at someone.	You never smile unless someone else smiles first.
It doesn't have to be a special occasion for you to give a gift.	You never give a gift unless someone gives you a gift first. Then, you give a gift of the same value.
You try to help solve problems.	You complain about others' problem-solving skills.
You always give your best effort during your practice and games.	You won't try any harder than anyone else does.
You are self-motivated.	You need constant praise to stay focused.
You say hi to someone you don't know while you're shopping.	When you see someone you don't know while you're shopping, you look away and pretend the person doesn't exist.
You ask someone who has fallen if he is okay.	When you see someone fall, you laugh at him.

From *Character-Building Activities: Teaching Responsibility, Interaction, and Group Dynamics* by Judy Demers, 2008, Champaign, IL: Human Kinetics.

References

Brown, H.J., & Spizman, R. (1996). *A hero in every heart.* Nashville, TN: Thomas Nelson.

Dennison, P.E., & Dennison, G. (1994). *Brain gym.* Teacher's edition revised. Ventura, CA: Edu-Kinesthetics, Inc.

Hellison, D. (1995). *Teaching responsibility through physical activity.* Champaign, IL: Human Kinetics.

Henderson, N. (2002). *The resiliency route to authentic self-esteem and life success.* Resiliency in Action, Inc. www.resiliency.com/htm/build.htm

Koehler, M.D., & Royer, K.E. (2001). *First class character education: Activities program. Ready-to-use lessons & activities for grades 7-12.* Paramus, NJ: Prentice Hall.

Scully, J.L. (2000). *The power of social skills in character development: helping diverse learners succeed.* Port Chester, NY: Dude Publishing.

Warner, M.J. (1999). *The complete idiot's guide to enhancing self-esteem.* Indianapolis, IN: Alpha Books.

Weinberg, R.S., & Gould, D. (1999). *Foundations of sport and exercise psychology.* Champaign, IL: Human Kinetics.

Suggested Readings

Ammon-Wexler, J. (2005). *Acquiring your self-image.* http://taletdevelop.com/articles/AYSI.html

APA Help Center. Health & Emotional Wellness. *Strategies for controlling your anger.* www.apahelpcenter.org/articles/article.php?id=30

Benson, P., Galbraith, J., & Espeland, P. (1998). *What kids need to succeed.* Minneapolis: Free Spirit.

Blaydes, J. (2002). *Advocacy: A case for daily quality physical education.* www.actionbasedlearning.com/cgi-bin/article.pl

California Task Force to Promote Self-esteem and Personal and Social Responsibility. (1990). *Toward a state of esteem.* California Department of Education.

Carr, R.A. (1996). *Positive peer pressure, a transition perspective.* Family Connections. B.C. Council for the Family.

Damon, W. (1995). *Greater expectations: Overcoming the culture of indulgence in our homes and schools.* New York, NY: Free Press Paperbacks.

Glover, D.R., & Anderson, L.A. (2003). *Character education: 43 fitness activities for community building.* Champaign, IL: Human Kinetics.

Grevious, S.C. (1999). *Teen smart! Ready-to-use activities to help teens build positive relationships with peers and adults.* West Nyack, NY: Center for Applied Research Education.

Herod, L. (1999). *Discovering me: A guide to teaching health and building adolescents' self-esteem.* Needham Heights, MA: Allyn & Bacon (a Pearson Education Company).

Hillman, J. (1996). *The soul's code: In search of character and calling.* New York, NY: Warner.

Huitt, W. (2003). *Important values for school-aged children and youth: A preliminary report.* Valdosta, GA: Valdosta State University.

Jenson, E. (1998). *Teaching with the brain in mind.* Association for Supervision and Curriculum Development.

KidsHealth. (1995-2006). The Nemours Foundation. http://kidshealth.org/kid/feeling/friend/peer_pressure.html and http://kidshealth.org/parent/emotions/feelings/self_esteem.html

King, D. (2001). *Exercise seen boosting children's brain function.* Boston Globe. Nov. 9, 1999.

Kretchmar, R. (2001). *Practical philosophy of sport.* Champaign, IL: Human Kinetics, 237.

Laughlin, N. (2006). *Character development in college sports.* Department of Exercise and Sport Science, University of San Francisco. *Journal of College and Character.* Vol. 2.

McKay, M., & Fanning, P. (2000). *Self-esteem: A proven program of cognitive technique for assessing, improving, and maintaining your self-esteem* (3rd ed.) New York, NY: MJF Books.

National Association for Sport and Physical Education. (Dec. 2002). *New study supports physically fit kids perform better academically.* www.aahperd.org/ naspe/template.cfm?template=pr_121002.html

National Center for Youth Issues. *Character counts: Making the right moves.* Presented by Matt Fischer, with permission from Dr. Thomas Lickona.

Oelstrom, T. (2003). *Building the dream house with a foundation of character.* Journal of College and Character. Vol. 2. www.collegevalues.org.

Permanente Medical Group. (2005). *Anger and hostility.* E-Handout #6307E (Revised 5-05) RL 9.5.

Reader's Digest Association. (1995). *Health and healing the natural way—the stress factor.* New York: General Books.

Sheldon, W.H., & Stevens, S.S. (1940). *The varieties of temperament.* New York: Harper.

Suomi, J., Collier, D., & Brown, L. (2003). Factors affecting the social experiences of students in elementary physical education classes. *Journal of Teaching in Physical Education, 22,* 186-202.

Toner, P.R. (1993). *Relationships and communication activities.* West Nyack, NY: Center for Applied Research in Education.

University of Texas at Austin. (1999). *Better self-esteem.* The Counseling & Mental Health Center.

Vigil, G., D'Alessandro, D., & Huth, L. (2002). *Teenagers and stress.* Virtual Pediatric Hospital. www.vitualpediatrichospital.org/patients/cqqa/teenager-sstress.shtml

Wack, B. (1991). *Motivating the unmotivated: Teaching self-motivation, self-discipline & responsibility.* Oakland, CA: Effective Learning Resources.

Yeager, J.M., Buxton, J.N., Baltzell, A.L., & Bzdell, W.B. (2001). *Character and coaching: Building virtue in athletic programs.* Port Chester, NY: Dude Publishing.

About the Author

Judy Demers currently teaches physical education at Castillero Middle School in San José, California. Demers developed the physical education curriculum for her individual classes and the San José Unified School District. She has written two professional improvement projects for San José Unified School District, one of which she presented at the California Association of Health, Physical Education, Recreation and Dance (CAHPERD) conference. She received her bachelor's and master's degrees from San José State University. Demers has also served on health and physical education task forces and the California Healthy Kids Material Review Board, and she helped design district standards. Demers has been a member of CAHPERD since 1995 and has been a member of the Bay Area Physical Education and Health Subject Matter Project for several years.